STRATEGIC LEARNING

STRATEGIC LEARNING

HOW TO BE SMARTER THAN YOUR COMPETITION AND TURN KEY INSIGHTS INTO COMPETITIVE ADVANTAGE

WILLIE PIETERSEN

WILEY

John Wiley & Sons, Inc.

Published by John Wiley & Sons, Inc., Hoboken, New Jersey.

Published simultaneously in Canada.

For general information on our other products and services or for technical support, please contact our Customer Care Department within the United States at (800) 762-2974, outside the United States at (317) 572-3993 or fax (317) 572-4002.

Wiley also publishes its books in a variety of electronic formats. Some content that appears in print may not be available in electronic books. For more information about Wiley products, visit our web site at www.wiley.com.

Library of Congress Cataloging-in-Publication Data:

Pietersen, Willie.
  Strategic learning : how to be smarter than your competition and turn key insights into competitive advantage / by Willie Pietersen.
      p. cm.
  Includes index.
  ISBN 978-0-470-54069-5 (cloth)
  1. Organizational learning.   2. Strategic planning.   3. Leadership.
4. Knowledge management. I.   Title.
HD58.82.P533 2010
658.4'038—dc22   2009042890

Printed in the United States of America

10 9 8 7 6 5 4 3

CONTENTS

ACKNOWLEDGMENTS   **XI**

INTRODUCTION   **XIII**
The New Competitive Context   xiv
Winning in the New Environment   xvi
Reinventing Strategy with Strategic Learning   xvi
Why This Book?   xviii
Getting to Excelling   xix

PART I WHAT EVERY ORGANIZATION NEEDS TO KNOW ABOUT STRATEGY   **1**

CHAPTER 1
The Real Job of Strategy   **3**
What Is Strategy?   5
What Key Questions Must Strategy Answer for Us?   6
Choice-Making in Action   8
Strategy and Planning Are Different   12
Closing the Doing/Excelling Gap   14

CHAPTER 2
Defining Competitive Advantage: How Much More Value Do You Deliver Than Your Competitors?   **15**
Mind the Gap   16

Stretching the Elastic Band 18
GM's Race to the Bottom 21
Value Leadership through a Winning Proposition 24
What's Your Winning Proposition? 26
The Moment of Truth 27

PART II APPLYING STRATEGIC LEARNING TO CREATE AN ADAPTIVE ENTERPRISE 31

CHAPTER 3
Strategic Learning: Four Key Steps, One Cycle 33
Do You Have a Robust Method? 34
What Were We Thinking? 35
The Theory of Natural Selection 37
Complexity Theory 39
Learning Organizations 39
Strategy's New Mission 40
The Five Killer Competencies 40
The Strategic Learning Cycle 41
What We've Learned from Deming 42
Building Capability through Deliberate Practice 43

CHAPTER 4
Learn: Using a Situation Analysis to Generate Superior Insights about Your External Environment and Your Own Realities 47
The "Sense and Respond" Imperative 48
Learning through the Situation Analysis 49
Analyzing Customer Needs 51
Who Are Our Stakeholders and Why Do They Matter? 59
Analyzing Competitors 63
Interpreting Industry Dynamics 66
Taking a Broader View 68
Facing Your Own Realities 69

Pulling Together the Situation Analysis   73
Winning the Battle for Insights   75
Doing a Great Situation Analysis: The Rules of Success 78

CHAPTER 5
**Focus: Clarifying Your Winning Proposition and Identifying
Your Key Priorities**   **81**
Making Your Strategic Choices   81
The Parmenides Fallacy   83
Value Proposition versus Winning Proposition   87
Where Does Your Vision Fit In?   90
Delivering Superior Profits   90
The Three Bottom Lines   93
Your Key Priorities   95
How the Girl Scouts Did It   99
Deciding What Not to Do   103

CHAPTER 6
Align: Mobilizing Your Entire Organization behind Your Strategy **109**
Leading a Journey   110
The Golden Rules of Successful Execution   112
Closing the Gaps   113
The Business Ecosystem   119
Changing an Organization's Culture   125
Avoiding the Values Trap   131

CHAPTER 7
Overcoming Resistance to Change and Driving Momentum **135**
Dealing with the Sources of Resistance   137
The Lessons of the Sigmoid Curve   138
The Curse of Success   139
Launching the Second Curve   142
Maximize Participation   146
Generate Short-Term Wins   149
Deal Directly with Resisters   150
Set a Shining Example   154

CHAPTER 8
Translating Your Strategy into a Compelling Leadership
Message   157
    What Is Leadership?   160
    Building a Cathedral   161
    Commander's Intent   162
    Who Are the Leaders?   163
    Developing Your Leadership Message   165
    The Power of Storytelling   167
    The Need for Repetition   169

CHAPTER 9
Execute: Implementing and Experimenting in the Strategic
Learning Cycle   171
    Learning through Experimentation   172
    Learning from Others   174
    Learning from Mistakes   175
    Experiential Learning: The After-Action Review   176
    Strategic Learning 365 Days a Year   179

PART III INTEGRATING STRATEGY AND LEADERSHIP   181

CHAPTER 10
Leading through a Crisis   183
    Dealing Successfully with the Unexpected   184
    Learning Your Way Out of a Crisis   186
    Building Readiness   188
    Seizing Opportunities during a Crisis   190
    The Human Dimension   191

CHAPTER 11
Becoming an Integrated Leader   195
    The Three Domains of Leadership   196
    Articulating Your Leadership Credo   199
    The Quest for Self-Knowledge   201
    The Lifeline Exercise   202
    Applying Strategic Learning to Yourself   206

CONCLUSION
The 5 Cs: Choices, Clarity, Change, Courage, and Compassion   211
    The Five Cs   213

APPENDIX   217

NOTES   219

INDEX   225

ACKNOWLEDGMENTS

Responsibility for the content and ideas in this book is entirely my own. However, I could not have written it without the dedicated and enthusiastic help from a great "supporting cast."

First of all, my thanks to Catherine Fredman for her expertise in helping me refine and polish the manuscript; for reminding me along the way about the importance of examples and stories; for her willingness to challenge me in the interests of providing clarity; and for bringing her keen professional eye to the organization and structure of the book.

Credit goes to my two accomplished reviewers, Jeff Kuhn and Karl Weber. Jeff and I often work together on Strategic Learning workshops, and both Jeff and Karl helped me on my first book, *Reinventing Strategy*. The two of them provided what I value most—thoughtful and unvarnished feedback—and the book is undoubtedly better for it.

Amy Deiner from Columbia Business School has been my tireless researcher. Amy attended diligently to the business of fact-checking and locating source reference material, and she brought a discerning intelligence to this important assignment. Thank you, Amy.

Thank you Karen Fisk for bringing an eagle-eye, and great sensibility to the exacting task of proofreading.

I owe a debt of gratitude to my literary agent, Judith Ehrlich. As she did on my first book, Judith caringly and methodically helped me navigate through all the contractual aspects.

Richard Narramore, senior editor at John Wiley & Sons, Inc., provided just the right blend of constructive guidance and creative freedom, and he did so with unfailing courtesy. Richard, production editor Lauren Freestone, and all the members of the Wiley team have been a pleasure to work with.

Finally, I'd like to say a special thank you to my executive assistant, Aimee Chu, for her hard work, loyalty, and dedication. It was Aimee's often thankless task to ensure that the manuscript was correctly formatted and to keep track of the various iterations of the text so that everything was efficiently organized. Aimee patiently took care of the hassles so that I could concentrate on the writing.

INTRODUCTION

The difficulty lies not in new ideas, but escaping the old ones, which penetrate every corner of our minds.
—JOHN MAYNARD KEYNES

No industry is immune from continuous change. Name any product or service and I'll guarantee that if it had a long lifespan, that lifespan is getting shorter. If it had a short lifespan, it is even more compressed. No barrier to competition remains safe.

The Army War College in Carlisle, Pennsylvania, often called "the school for generals," has coined an acronym for an environment in flux: VUCA, for *volatile, uncertain, complex, and ambiguous.* The term also applies to today's business landscape. It's not only that the specific cyclical and structural elements of today's environment are different, but that they are more volatile, uncertain, complex, and ambiguous than ever before.

Beyond the shock to the system of the recent financial crisis and deep recession that followed—foreseen by hardly anyone—there are deep, ongoing mutations that are revolutionizing the way business is done. The list of changes is a familiar one: profound demographic shifts; the Asian economic advancement; the development of resource nationalism; the growing influence of nongovernment organizations (NGOs), and regulatory changes in banking, energy, healthcare, and food safety. The list goes on. Abetting all these forces are two overarching factors that are producing a transformative impact in their own right: the rapid development of information technology and globalization, and the massive power of these two forces working together.

The consequences of this VUCA environment are being felt by everyone. The shelf life of any advantage is constantly shrinking; competitive intensity is escalating; pricing and profit margins are under pressure; and there is a premium on speed, flexibility, and innovation. In industry after industry that I work with I hear the same refrain: The environment is getting tougher. Global competitors are everywhere. They are faster, more innovative, and more efficient. It's harder than ever to find a competitive advantage; even harder to sustain it. As one CEO in the healthcare industry said to me, "The era of easy money is over. We can no longer rely on product superiority alone. We have to master operational effectiveness, too."

The result is, we now have to play an "and" game. You no longer have a choice between being a low-cost operator or a great innovator; you have to excel at both low costs *and* superior customer solutions. If you dwell just on superior customer benefits, then lower costs and a more efficient supply chain will kill you. Conversely, if you focus just on lower costs but don't pay attention to the needs of customers, *that* will kill you.

The aim of this book is not to rehash the grainy details of the various changes that are happening around us. The particulars of these will vary from industry to industry. Rather, my purpose is to help clarify the *essential nature* of this new environment, and then to address what I believe is the larger question: *What should be our response to it?*

The New Competitive Context

To understand the fundamentals of today's competitive landscape, it helps to view it in an historical context. When we examine the long-term trends, we can see four big revolutions, each of which ushered

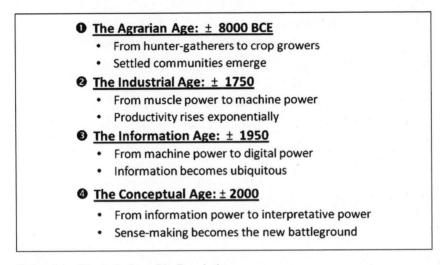

❶ **The Agrarian Age: ± 8000 BCE**
  • From hunter-gatherers to crop growers
  • Settled communities emerge

❷ **The Industrial Age: ± 1750**
  • From muscle power to machine power
  • Productivity rises exponentially

❸ **The Information Age: ± 1950**
  • From machine power to digital power
  • Information becomes ubiquitous

❹ **The Conceptual Age: ± 2000**
  • From information power to interpretative power
  • Sense-making becomes the new battleground

Figure I.1 History's Four Big Revolutions

in a new era, with totally new challenges and rules for success: the agrarian age, the industrial age, the information age, and our current era—what writer and trend-watcher Daniel Pink has called the "conceptual age" (see Figure I.1).[1]

Note the pace of change. The agrarian age lasted almost 10,000 years, the industrial age 200 years, and the information age 50 years. The conceptual age is only 10 years old.

The change from the information age to the conceptual age has been a radical one. The information age concentrated on the volume and ubiquity of data. It turned information into a commodity, which has become abundant, cheap, and rapidly transferable. In the conceptual age, our source of competitive advantage is no longer finding more information; it is making sense of the overwhelming volume of information already available to us. Sense-making, creativity, and the ability to synthesize, not just analyze, have become paramount.

To succeed in this new world, organizations will need to manage a fundamental shift to a different leadership model, as shown in Figure I.2. Competition in every arena and on every level is affected by these changes.

Whenever the environment shifts in a dramatic way, some species become extinct, while others adapt and thrive. Adapting and

Discipline	⟶	Adaptiveness
Planning	⟶	Discovery
Hard Assets	⟶	Knowledge
Structure	⟶	Process
Controls	⟶	Values
Inside-Out	⟶	Outside-In
Size	⟶	Speed
Management	⟶	Leadership

Figure I.2 Fundamental Shifts

thriving in these changing competitive circumstances is going to be extremely challenging and will produce a whole new set of winners and losers.

Winning in the New Environment

What does all this mean for organizational leaders? The answer is the same whether we are engaged in developing national policy, military campaigns, or strategies for commercial or not-for-profit enterprises; and for organizations large and small. Our key leadership challenge is to build adaptive organizations—those with an ingrained ability to make sense of the changing environment, and then rapidly translate these insights into action.

This thought is not new. In fact, it has become something of a rallying cry. We hear it repeatedly in books, speeches, and business articles. But the rhetoric is easy. What has been missing is a practical process to translate this transforming idea into practice.

Reinventing Strategy with Strategic Learning

The way that work gets done in organizations is through systematic processes. Concerted action is not an ad hoc affair. And it certainly does not result from simple exhortations, no matter how often or loudly they are repeated.

The processes we use must be fit for purpose: They must do the job they are designed to do. The old, ritualistic, numbers-based planning methods no longer work today. They were designed for a different, more static era. They are, simply, no longer fit for purpose. In a VUCA environment, our emphasis must shift to insights, ideas, and ongoing renewal. What is necessary is a dynamic method for creating winning strategies and renewing those strategies as the environment changes. We must change our approach from "strategy as planning" to "strategy as learning."

Eight years ago, in my first book, *Reinventing Strategy*, I laid out a process called Strategic Learning, a practical leadership method for translating these ideas into action. Strategic Learning is a learning-based process for creating and implementing breakthrough strategies. But unlike traditional strategy, which aims at producing one-time change, Strategic Learning drives continuous adaptation.

As shown in Figure I.3, the process has four linked action steps—*Learn, Focus, Align,* and *Execute*—which build on one another and are repeated (as a fifth step) in a continuous cycle. In essence, Strategic Learning is an "insight to action" model. The leadership challenge is to repeat it over and over, so that an organization continuously learns from its own actions and from scanning the environment, and then modifies its strategies accordingly. Strategic

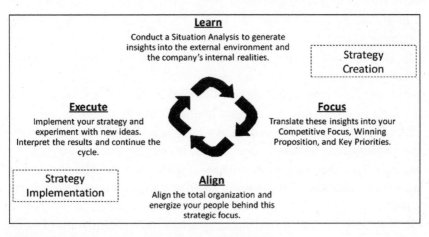

Figure I.3   Strategic Learning: The Leadership Process

Learning combines strategy, learning, and leadership in one unified process.

The underlying ideas and tools of Strategic Learning have since been applied in organizations as wide-ranging as ExxonMobil, Ericsson, DePuy, Novartis, the Federal Home Loan Bank of Atlanta, the Girl Scouts of the USA, and Henry Schein, Inc., among others. The leaders I have worked with feel that the process and the concepts that have inspired it are intrinsically compelling and have made a real difference to their organizations. The Strategic Learning methodology has also become the basis for how strategy is taught at Columbia Business School's Executive Education programs.

Why This Book?

The past eight years have served as an "action learning" laboratory. Through my seminars and consulting work, there have been multiple opportunities to apply the principles of continuous learning to the Strategic Learning process. It has been tested in the white heat of the action arena, subjected to intellectual scrutiny and debate by organizational leaders and my colleagues at Columbia University, and assessed in the light of my own experience as a practitioner. Both I and the organizations applying the Strategic Learning process have discovered how to derive better and better results from it. We have learned through trial and error what works and what doesn't, and which concepts and tools can best help us adapt and excel in the evolving external environment in which we operate.

That's good, because compared to eight years ago, there is a greater need than ever for a process that enables organizations to make sense of and adapt to the VUCA environment, and do that better than competitors. It also is a healthy reminder that as we keep raising the bar on performance, we must address two gaps: The first is from knowing to doing. That gets us going, but doesn't carry us far enough. The second, and even more significant gap, is from doing to excelling. Addressing the doing/excelling gap is a journey that never stops.

It is in the spirit of our mutual pursuit of excellence that I write this book. In service of those who are already applying Strategic

Learning, I have now incorporated all my latest thinking, enriched by fresh examples and more extensive practical guidelines, which I hope will significantly enhance your effectiveness. For those who are new to Strategic Learning, this book will, I hope, introduce you to a set of ideas that you will find valuable and timely—ideas that you can readily translate into practice. In service of both groups of readers, I have pulled everything together in one place so that it will not be necessary to read the first book in order to get full value from the second.

Getting to Excelling

In the journey from doing to excelling, six key lessons, which I will emphasize in this book, have emerged about the effective application of Strategic Learning:

1. *To find great answers, we must discover great questions.* It is not possible to address the changing environment with all the right answers. The real challenge is to find the right questions. In fact, producing answers without the right questions can be downright dangerous.

   Entrenched answers create fixed mental models. They become a substitute for critical thinking. And, inevitably, they—and the organizations clinging to them—get overtaken by events. The right questions force us to challenge our underlying assumptions. They unfreeze us and open new vistas. Good questions open the doorway to insight; they serve as our portals of discovery. They help us adapt to change.

2. *Simplicity is the springboard for success.* I constantly challenge and cajole executives to express their strategy in as few words as possible, and then pare it down further to its absolute essence. When I hear the response, "It's more complicated than that," what I think is, "You don't understand it well enough." When you really understand something, you can simplify it. When you don't, you complicate it.

   Simplicity is not a short cut. It is hard work that goes to the very heart of effective leadership. Organizations cannot follow complexity. They are paralyzed by it. The task is to translate your strategy into a simple, compelling leadership message that will win the hearts and minds of all your people in support of what needs to be done. Most important, simplicity creates an intense focus on the right things, the crucial ingredient for success.

3. *Strategy means thinking from the outside-in.* What happens when co-workers get together for a friendly conversation? Most of the time, they talk about themselves: who's who in the zoo, who's doing what to whom, why so and so was promoted or not promoted, and so on. It's all about *us*—our team, our organization, our culture, our bosses. This is a natural state of affairs. But organizations that aim to become adaptive have to get used to an unnatural act: outside-in thinking.

   Outside-in thinking means the conversation starts with the competitive environment *outside* the organization: Who are our customers? What do they value most? What are our competitors doing? What are the key industry trends that might affect how we make money? Thinking strategically means thinking with that outside-in mind-set. Functioning strategically means making decisions based on that mind-set.

   The leap from knowing and doing to excelling takes place in the space between the challenges of the external environment and our internal abilities to meet them.

4. *The point of strategy is to win the battle for value creation.* There is a great deal of confusion about the key deliverable of a strategy. The result is that the outputs are often bland, all-embracing statements—meandering lists of what the organization plans to do. They amount to one-size-fits-all declarations that could be equally well applied to an organization's competitors.

   Such pronouncements are useless. In a competitive environment, everything is comparative. Customers have choices. The question is: *Why should they choose to do business with you?* The same applies to investors: *Why should they decide to give you their money?* Competing successfully means providing a margin of difference in the value you offer these two key stakeholders.

In short, strategy must define how an organization will win the competition for value creation. This means creating greater value for its customers and investors than the competing alternatives. Without a clear statement of how it will achieve such an aim—what I call a Winning Proposition—an organization cannot claim to have a strategy.

5. *Strategy is everyone's job.* I am often asked, "Whose job is it to create the strategy for an organization?" The answer that is expected is, "The top leadership, of course."

That answer is wrong. It is based on an outdated "command and control" philosophy. The truth is that it is everyone's job. The senior leaders, of course, have a crucial role: They must define the direction and strategic goals of the organization. But that's not where it stops. That's where it *starts*. It is the leadership responsibility of each manager at every level in an organization to create a clear line of sight to the organization's overarching goals, and then to translate those into a winning strategy for his or her domain of responsibility.

The logic is simple and unforgiving. It's a matter of strategic cohesion. If an organization is to win at value, then every subgroup in that organization must contribute to that value generation, or simply be a cost drag. There's nothing in between.

6. *Strategy and leadership are essential parts of each other.* Strategy does not have a life of its own. It is an inseparable part of leadership.

Leadership comprises three key domains:

▼ Intrapersonal leadership—leadership of self

▼ Strategic leadership—leadership of the organization

▼ Interpersonal leadership—leadership of others

The key to success is integrated leadership, ensuring that all three domains are working hand in hand, each one supporting the others. When any one is missing, the others cannot succeed.

All these lessons add up to one overarching epiphany: the importance of the human dimension. Of course, this is not news. Leaders constantly declare that "our people are our strongest asset." I ran companies for 20 years and know from personal experience that the difference between commitment and mere compliance is monumental. But the more I explore the potential of the Strategic Learning process, the more I am struck by the crucial role of the human spirit. It is *the* governing factor in the success or failure of any organization, or indeed any individual.

Napoleon, who is acknowledged to be the most successful military leader in modern history, was supposedly asked which was more important: material or spiritual resources? His answer: spiritual resources—by a factor of three to one. I don't know whether the story is apocryphal, but from my own experience running large organizations, I believe the ratio is absolutely right. In the final analysis, our leadership mission is to bring out the best in ourselves and each other. If we can't win hearts and minds, the greatest strategy in the world won't go anywhere, let alone help our organizations advance from knowing to doing to excelling.

What Every Organization Needs to Know about Strategy

1

The Real Job of Strategy

Our lives are the sum of the choices we make.

—Albert Camus

O rganizations create their futures through the strategies they pursue. These strategies may be developed in a thoughtful and systematic way or allowed to emerge haphazardly in a series of random, ad hoc decisions made in response to daily pressures. But one way or another, the strategy a company follows—that is, the choices it makes—determines its likely success. And in today's fast-changing environment, the ability to generate winning strategies, develop the tools to apply them, and mobilize employee commitment—not once but repeatedly—is more important than ever.

Yet astonishingly few executives, let alone the rank and file, are able to explain their company's strategy in a clear and compelling way. The trouble is that strategy is a largely misunderstood and misapplied concept. Somehow, there's a notion that strategy is complex

3

and mysterious, something best left to gurus and experts. Actually, the opposite is true. It's not at all arcane. In fact, it's dead simple, and therein lies its power.

It's puzzling that so few companies have devoted sufficient time or energy to clarifying the nature of strategy or to creating an effective, organization-wide method for developing winning strategies. Instead, many of them plunge directly into strategy formulation on impulse, without defining a clear process. It's as if the manager of an auto assembly plant were to dump a load of parts onto the factory floor and tell the workers, "Here, make some cars," without defining a manufacturing process with the end product in mind.

The penalties for this lack of strategic leadership are considerable. A survey of 336 organizations by Right Management Consultants found that two-thirds of employees do not know or understand their company's strategy.[1] A poll of 23,000 employees highlighted by Stephen Covey paints a similarly disturbing picture:[2]

▼ Only 37 percent said they have a clear understanding of what their organization is trying to achieve, and why.

▼ Only 20 percent were enthusiastic about their team's and their organization's goals.

▼ Only 20 percent said they had a clear "line of sight" between their tasks and their organization's goals.

It is hard to imagine how such companies can hope to survive and thrive with this lack of clarity and employee alignment on strategic direction. In fact, the evidence shows that the ability of organizations to maintain success in our VUCA (volatile, uncertain, complex and ambiguous) environment is inexorably declining. A survey of Fortune 1000 companies since 1973 found that between 1973 and 1983, 35 percent of the top 20 names were new (see Figure 1.1). The number rose to 45 percent in the following decade, and between 1993 and 2003, shot up to 60 percent.[3]

This state of affairs suggests that one of the highest hurdles facing organizational leaders today is their inability to mobilize their companies behind strategies that create and sustain competitive advantage.

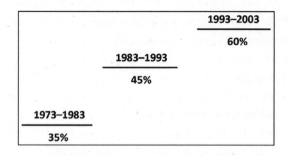

Figure 1.1   Fortune 1000 Companies: Percent New in Top 20
Source: Edward E. Lawler III and Chris Worley, *Built to Change: How to Achieve Sustained Organizational Effectiveness* (Jossey-Bass, 2006).

The primary aim of this book is to offer a practical and proven method for creating and implementing winning strategies, and renewing those strategies as the environment changes. But this process—Strategic Learning—is not just a step-by-step ritual. It is inspired by a set of crucial underlying ideas. The key to the successful application of Strategic Learning is to understand and mobilize these key concepts.

To clarify our thinking, we need to answer two important questions:

▼ What is strategy?

▼ What key questions must strategy answer for us?

Let's examine each of these questions.

What Is Strategy?

Aristotle said, "We do not know a truth without knowing its cause." Following Aristotle's logic, the best way to understand the real meaning of strategy is to understand its origins. Where does it come from? Why does it exist? What is so compelling about it?

What gave birth to strategy was the need to respond to two inescapable realities: the fact that we have limited resources, and the inevitability of competition. These stark realities force organizations to make choices on how best to use their scarce resources for the achievement of competitive advantage. The purpose of this choice-making is to create an intense focus on the few things that matter most to an organization's success.

Strategy is, simply, the sum of an organization's choices about where it will compete, how it will create superior value for its customers, and how it will generate superior returns to its investors. In a world of limited resources, a company that tries to be all things to all people, with no specific focus or direction, will soon squander its resources and either fall behind its competitors or go out of business.

Consider this: If you had unlimited resources, there would be no requirement for a strategy because there would be no need to decide what *not* to do. You could eliminate all risk by endlessly piling on resources, just in case your choices were wrong. You could survive indefinitely by throwing time and money and people at your problems until your obstacles and competitors are utterly overwhelmed. But in the real world, there is no such thing as unlimited resources. Even the world's greatest corporations have only so much cash, so many employees, so many factories.

The way that competition expresses itself is through the interaction of choices in the marketplace. The smartest choices, well executed, will win the game.

What Key Questions Must Strategy Answer for Us?

What do the key deliverables of strategy look like? If it is to create value, strategy must provide a good return on the time and effort we put into it.

A successful strategy is not just a matter of open-ended choice-making. It is choice-making in service of answering some specific and very important questions. The answers to these questions will determine your destiny.

To clarify what these questions are and why they are important, let's go back for a moment to the origins of strategy. Strategy was originally a military concept. The word is derived from the Greek *strategia*, meaning "generalship," which itself is compounded from two words, *stratos*, meaning "army," and *agein*, "to lead." (Note the implicit connection between strategy and leadership, a theme to which I'll return throughout this book.)

Now let's indulge in a little military role-playing.

Imagine that you are the leader of a country—let's call it country A. Assume that for good and sound reasons, country A is faced with the unpleasant prospect of going to war against country B. You have asked your experts to study and compare the resources available to your country and country B. There are disparities, relative strengths and weaknesses, that call for a really smart approach to conducting this war.

Faced with this challenge, you call a cabinet meeting and ask your most senior general to be in attendance. You discuss the relative resources available to your country and country B. The general assures you that he has done his homework on this. Now you ask the big question that every good general must be able to answer: "General, how will we win?"

But if he is a good general, he will refuse to answer your question, until you have provided a clear answer to *his* question: "What is your aim?" What do you want to achieve by going to war? Is it regime change? Is it disarmament? Is it nation-building? The point is, you can't figure out how you will win until you define what kind of contest you are involved in.

Let's translate this role-play into a business context. Of course, there are differences between warfare and business strategy. War is a matter of life and death, and wars are typically zero-sum encounters. But this military example clarifies some key principles about any kind of strategy.

The first and most crucial point is that a strategy must define how you will win. This concept is not exclusive to warfare. On this point we must be clear: *Winning in business means winning at value.* That is a central theme of this book.

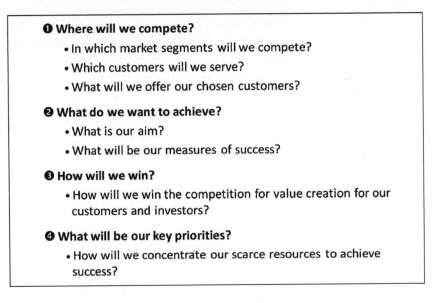

❶ Where will we compete?
- In which market segments will we compete?
- Which customers will we serve?
- What will we offer our chosen customers?

❷ What do we want to achieve?
- What is our aim?
- What will be our measures of success?

❸ How will we win?
- How will we win the competition for value creation for our customers and investors?

❹ What will be our key priorities?
- How will we concentrate our scarce resources to achieve success?

Figure 1.2   The Key Questions Strategy Must Answer

Second, the military role-play clarifies the questions that must be asked in the process of strategic choice-making for any enterprise. It is the answers to these questions that make your strategy specific, clear, and actionable.

Here, then, in Figure 1.2, are the key questions every organization must answer in the process of creating a strategy.

Military analyst Antoine Jomini writes that strategy is the concentration of mass upon decisive points. It's the same in business. Answering these questions forces an enterprise to make its critical strategic choices and thereby harness the power of concentration. The ultimate purpose of a strategy is to create clarity of focus. This, in turn, is the essential platform for leadership effectiveness.

Choice-Making in Action

The contest playing out between Boeing and Airbus in the commercial aviation business provides a dramatic example of how each company has dealt with the challenges of high-stakes choice-making.

Boeing and Airbus manufacture aircraft for commercial carriers such as Continental Airlines, United, Singapore Airlines, and others. They compete against each other in the same key markets and with a similar portfolio of planes. Measured by size, range, fuel efficiency, and operational reliability, for example, there is not a major difference between a Boeing 737 and an Airbus A320. As the new millennium dawned, each company looked for a development that would conclusively give it a competitive advantage.

Boeing had actually captured such an advantage decades before, when it introduced the large, more comfortable, 747. The Concorde, although a financial disaster, was another plane that clearly changed the flying experience for passengers, persuading an affluent group of people to choose British Airways or Air France just to enjoy the benefits of this supersonic plane.

Now, both Airbus and Boeing were determined to develop an operationally efficient, more passenger-pleasing aircraft that would have the same disruptive qualities as the Concorde. Boeing actually called this futuristic plane "the game changer."

The crucial question each company faced was, in a game of bet and counterbet, which particular choice would eclipse the other player? Should it be a large-capacity plane best suited to the hub-and-spoke market, like an updated 747? Or should it aim its new entry mainly at the point-to point routes that avoid connecting between busy airport hubs? Which segment was likely to have the most growth in the future, and what kind of plane would create the greatest value for the airlines and their customers in that segment? Of course, these alternatives have certain elements in common, but in terms of their core benefits they are different, and therefore so is their likely growth potential.

Boeing has placed its bet on the point-to-point market. Its new entry will be the 787, designed to carry about 250 passengers, which it has dubbed the Dreamliner. With a new generation of fuel-efficient engines and a skin made largely from carbon-reinforced plastic, the plane represents an exciting technological breakthrough. Carbon-fiber composites such as this routinely strengthen tennis rackets and parts of fighter planes, but had never been used on such a large scale. The 787's transformational technology enhances the customer experience with improved air quality inside the cabin, and bigger windows, as well as, according to Boeing, making the plane 20 percent less expensive to operate and a third less expensive to maintain than its competitive equivalents. The list price is stated to be about $150 million per plane.

Airbus, meanwhile, placed its bet on the hub-and-spoke market with the huge A380. Carrying approximately 555 passengers—more than 100 over the Boeing 747 passenger limit and twice the number of the Dreamliner—the A380 is configured to incorporate lounges and stratospheric shopping malls to relieve the tedium of long flights, and its enormous size promises significant efficiencies in operating costs. The list price is close to $300 million per plane.

This case illustrates the challenges of choice-making in the development of a strategy. Let's put ourselves in the shoes of Boeing and Airbus at the time when they had to make these decisions. The development costs were reportedly calculated at $8 billion for the Dreamliner and $12 billion for the A380 *before* cost overruns (which we know in retrospect have been considerable at both companies). Based on these parameters, which was the smarter choice? Wouldn't it be nice if these companies had unlimited resources and could just do both? Obviously, that was not possible. A choice had to be made. And that epitomizes the issue strategy must address: We can't do it all.

It is too early to tell whether Boeing or Airbus has made the better bet. All will depend on the comparative benefits perceived by the airlines and their flying customers. When the final story gets told, it will boil down to which company had the sharpest insights into the needs of its customers and the key trends in the industry.

The same principles apply in every sphere, from business to education to not-for-profit organizations to government.

Think about running a country. A government is constantly having to make choices and trade-offs on where it will spend its resources. There is a continuous tug-of-war between competing needs such as healthcare, housing, education, national security, transportation, and so on. The government can raise the necessary revenue in only two ways: through taxes and borrowing. Both of these options are limited.

I was born in South Africa and return there once a year. It is a beautiful and enchanting place. Now that it has achieved democracy, its greatest challenge is to generate enough economic growth to pay for the enormous gaps in human welfare that still exist. My opinion is that the country's great economic opportunity lies in the development of tourism. It has an ideal climate, friendly people, wonderful beaches, stunning game parks, and a fantastic landscape. What is the big spoiler? Too much crime.

After a recent visit, my wife, Laura, and I were sitting in the Cape Town airport awaiting our flight back to the United States and reminiscing about the wonderful time we had had. As we glanced through the local newspaper, we saw a story citing the grim statistics about crime. The government had already launched a campaign to combat this problem, but clearly much more needed to be done. I felt a surge of frustration about what I saw as a lack of adequate resources being applied to deal more decisively with this scourge. I put down my newspaper and exclaimed to Laura, "Why don't they simply hire and train thousands more policemen and put them on the streets?"

"Okay, Mr. Professor," she replied, "let me tell you why: because they don't have unlimited funds. The money would have to come out of the healthcare budget or housing or education or fighting AIDS. They have to make trade-offs. Isn't this what you teach?"

Exactly so.

These are examples of some of the large individual bets that companies and governments often have to make. Managers at every level face smaller but equally significant choices every day. Which of these questions sound familiar? China and India are growing rapidly, and our competitors are moving in; which of these geographies should we enter? Which market segments should we concentrate on? Which products should we offer? Which R&D projects should we back? Which should we discontinue? Strategically coherent organizations make these choices based on a clear set of strategic parameters, so that the *sum* of their choices represents a consistent expression of that strategy.

Why we need a strategy
- Limited resources
- Competitors

The main purpose of strategy
- Making the best choices
- Creating clarity of focus

The questions it must answer
- Where will we compete?
- What is our aim?
- How will we win?

The measure of success: Value creation
- Greater value for our customers
- Superior profits for our company

Figure 1.3 The Essence of Strategy

One point must be stressed: There is no such thing as a non-choice. Doing nothing is itself an implicit choice, and acts of omission have consequences just as profound as acts of commission.

Figure 1.3 summarizes the key points we have covered.

Strategy and Planning Are Different

To complete our understanding of what strategy is, we also need to clarify what it is not. One source of confusion concerns the difference between strategy and planning. Many executives struggle to distinguish between the two and end up in no-man's-land.

The important fact is that there are fundamental differences between strategy and planning, and these differences matter a great deal (see Figure 1.4).

Strategy is about doing the right things. It involves making the most intelligent choices; it clarifies where an organization will compete and how it will win the competition for value creation; and it creates an intense focus on the few things that matter most.

Planning, on the other hand, concerns doing things right. It provides orderliness, discipline, and logistical rigor; its purpose is not to

Strategy: About Doing the Right Things
- Determines where to compete and how to win
- Is about making the best choices
- Creates an intense focus on the vital few

Planning: About Doing Things Right
- Provides orderliness and discipline
- Is about putting strategy into action, not making it
- Creates forecasts, logistics, and budgets

Figure 1.4 Strategy and Planning Are Completely Different Things

produce breakthrough thinking, but predictability; and it generates forecasts, blueprints, and budgets.

A good way to understand the difference between strategy and planning is to think about running a railroad company: Strategy defines where you will lay the railroad tracks; planning ensures that the trains run on time.

I am not arguing that planning is not important. Both strategy and planning are vital, but one is not a substitute for the other. If the railroad tracks go to all the wrong destinations, it doesn't help that the trains get you there on time. Conversely, getting the destinations right but always arriving late would be equally dysfunctional. Both have to be in place to run a successful railroad.

Because their outputs are so different, combining strategy and planning into one process is a toxic mixture. The evidence suggests that such a combination is likely to produce 90 percent planning and only 10 percent strategy. Planning becomes a substitute for strategy. Over time, such companies and their people will lose the ability to think and act strategically.

The golden rule is: strategy first, and planning afterwards.

Because clarity about the essence of strategy is so important, and we will be building on this understanding in future chapters, let me reiterate our definition of strategy, in Figure 1.5.

An organization's strategy harnesses insight to make choices on where it will compete, what it will offer, and how it will win by generating greater value for its customers and superior profits for the enterprise.

The key job of strategy is to create an intense focus on the few things that matter most.

Figure 1.5 What Is Strategy?

Closing the Doing/Excelling Gap

Effective strategic leadership is one of our greatest challenges in today's VUCA environment. As I mentioned in the Introduction, just moving from knowing to doing is not enough. In the next chapters, we'll explore how to *excel* at creating and implementing your strategy.

Defining Competitive Advantage

How Much More Value Do You Deliver Than Your Competitors?

The future never just happened. It was created.

—Will Durant

The centerpiece of any strategy is encapsulated in an organization's Winning Proposition. If an organization can't define its Winning Proposition in a simple and compelling way, it cannot claim to have a strategy.

What does *winning* mean?

Does it mean your ability to survive? Does it mean keeping your shareholders happy? Does it mean providing benefits for your customers and stakeholders and the communities in which you live and operate? Does it mean having the largest market share?

Winning encompasses all of these things, but to take it out of the realm of slogans we need a rigorous measure that tells us unambiguously whether we are winning or not. This can be distilled to one simple test: a Winning Proposition must clearly produce a competitive advantage for your organization.

Unfortunately, "competitive advantage" is one of those buzz phrases that has become a substitute for thought. We have all heard executives proclaiming proudly that their organizations have a competitive advantage without offering any clear explanation of what that means. The fact is that competitive advantage is very tangible and can be evaluated, so there need be no speculation about whether it exists. In fact, I would argue that it is the single most important gauge of organizational success. To clarify this assessment, we need to define exactly what we mean by competitive advantage.

The underlying idea is that in a competitive environment, everything is comparative. Absolutes have no meaning. If we hear that an Olympic athlete has run the 100-meter race in 9.8 seconds, this tells us very little (unless he or she was the only runner). But if we hear the athlete won the gold medal, this tells us everything. The same is true in business.

Now, let me pose a question. In attaining competitive advantage, which is more important: providing unique benefits for customers or achieving superior operational effectiveness?

This question is a trap. Clearly, the one without the other (at least to some degree) is not the answer. The temptation is to say *both* and be done with it. But while both are true, that answer is incomplete and therefore misleading. Doing both obviously is necessary, but it's not sufficient. The real answer is that competitive advantage lies in the *difference* between the two. It's the gap that says it all.

Mind the Gap

If you have ever visited London, you probably have had the experience of riding on the London underground railway system. When a train pulls into a station and the doors open, a loud announcement echoes along the platform. Three short words caution passengers to

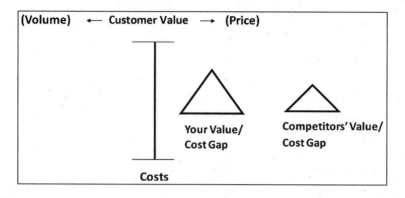

Figure 2.1 Achieving Competitive Advantage

watch their step as they get on and off the train, to avoid tripping in the space between the train and the platform: "MIND THE GAP!"

Competitive advantage in a business entails exactly the same injunction: Mind the gap! There are many gaps you ignore at your peril. At its most fundamental, though, competitive advantage means achieving a bigger gap than your competitors between the value your customers see in your product and the costs you incur in providing that product.

This gap is not a matter of subjective opinion. It can be objectively assessed, as Figure 2.1 illustrates.

As this diagram shows, you achieve competitive advantage if your value/cost gap is bigger than that of your competitors. Let's briefly examine the elements involved in this simple measure. Value can be described as the numerator, and costs as the denominator.

The denominator (costs) is straightforward. Any organization can—and should—regularly benchmark its costs against those of its competitors. Published data, supported by good analysis, can be relied upon to produce a well-grounded comparison. This is not particularly difficult. It is done all the time.

But what about the numerator? How do you compare the value your organization creates against your competitors? The crucial point to understand is that there is a dynamic interaction between value, price, and volume. Value is the driver—the prime mover, if you like. Price and volume are *derivatives of value*; they have no independent existence. So to assess the amount of value you are creating, look at its outputs: price and volume. This is the ultimate gauge of the amount of value you are generating.

How do you measure whether you are producing *superior* customer value? Rather than just claiming it, you can assess it. When you are generating greater value than your competition, you can either charge a premium price without sacrificing volume, or you can improve market share at comparable prices. If you are losing on value, then both volume and price will be under pressure, and one or both will be falling. Market share does not have a life of its own; it's a child of customer value. Similarly, price does not have an independent existence; it, too, is a derivative of value. This logic is ruthless: Your customers will convey it to you very loudly in very simple terms. Customers will buy more of your offerings, or pay you a higher price for them, only if they place a higher value on them than the competing alternatives. And, of course, the reverse is also painfully true.

Take SAP, the giant business software company, which has achieved high market shares in its chosen segments. SAP offers integrated solutions designed to improve efficiencies across its customers' entire supply chains, an enormously valuable benefit in today's world of global supply chains. SAP's destiny depends on its continuing ability to deliver superior results on this promise. If it begins to falter on delivering superior value, it would see the consequences either in falling market shares or lower prices versus competitors. The signals would be unmistakable.

Granted, the value comparison is not as precise as the cost comparison. But absolute precision is not the objective here. This is a diagnostic measure, which will tell you unarguably whether you are winning or losing on value.

Stretching the Elastic Band

How can you improve your competitive advantage? Think of an elastic band stretched between value and costs (see Figure 2.2). The wider you can stretch this elastic band, the greater your competitive advantage and the larger the amount of profit being generated.

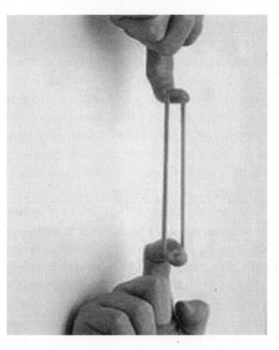

Figure 2.2 The Elastic Band between Value and Costs

Many businesses are tempted to compete on efficiency alone, and constantly stress operational effectiveness as a cure-all. In many ways, this is an easy way out. If you want to reduce costs, competitors can't stop you. But when you compete on costs, you are really competing only against yourself. Winning on value is much tougher. You have to outcompete your rivals.

Competing on costs is a requirement for staying in the game. Creating superior value is a necessity for winning the game. The key, of course, is to pull both upward and downward on the elastic band. Knowing where and how to stretch the band are strategic decisions that ultimately decide the difference between you and your competitors.

Take a look at the airline industry. Many of the big carriers fly the same type of aircraft to the same destinations in similar time slots with comparable safety records. With all this sameness, there is no basis for creating competitive advantage, right? Wrong. Airlines such as Virgin Atlantic and Singapore Airlines are able systematically to charge a price premium over their competition. Why? Simply because they concentrate on understanding the most important needs of their customers and on delivering a better all-round experience, consistently. We know they are creating greater value, because their customers are paying them more. We can't argue with the facts.

Cemex, the international cement company based in Mexico (which recently ran into difficulties for financial engineering, not operating reasons), achieved competitive advantage by pulling the elastic upward. Its costs per ton are similar to its largest global competitor, Holcim, but its price per ton is much higher.[1] Cemex provides higher value through a superb just-in-time system for cement deliveries that keeps construction projects humming along without delays, a major economic benefit. Cemex's customers agree, and are willing to pay a higher price.

There is, in the final analysis, no such thing as a commodity. Many people might consider cement or an airline trip to be a commodity, but these examples prove otherwise. To be sure, you can try to compete on price, but price cuts can be quickly neutralized, and the net effect is to transfer profits to customers. What companies like Cemex, Virgin Atlantic, and Singapore Airlines demonstrate is that when you consider the total customer experience, not just the underlying product, you can always find ways of generating superior value. To call your product or service a commodity is to abandon the pursuit of value, and hence the pursuit of competitive advantage.

A second point is that it is *perceived* value that counts. A brand is a perception of value in the mind of the customer. The customer's subjective reality is your objective reality.

Consider the following example: In the mid-1980s, Hitachi and General Electric jointly owned a factory in England that made identical TV sets. The only difference was the brand names on those sets. Through superior image building, which created greater trust in the minds of customers, the Hitachi units sold for $75 more than the GE sets, and sold twice as many![2] That's what prompted GE to get out of the TV set business. It would never be able to match Hitachi's profitability because it had lost the game on the perception of value.

When you think about it, you can never win by competing on price alone. The customer won't let you. In the customer's mind, you are competing on the relationship between price and value. This is true whether you acknowledge it or not. As Warren Buffet has pointed out, value is what customers get, and price is what they pay in return.[3] The two are inextricably connected.

GM's Race to the Bottom

Cautionary tales teach us as well. One of the most instructive examples I know is the sad story of General Motors' inexorable death march—a cautionary tale with few equals in the scale of its value destruction. This was not a sudden, unexpected event; it was a saga that played out over about 40 years. The causes of the misery were not hidden. They were starkly visible. And yet GM seemed strangely incapable of addressing the reality that was slowly killing it.

In its prime, GM boasted more than 50 percent of the U.S. auto market.[4] It seemed unassailable. Its array of brands, as its advertisements proclaimed, matched "every purse and purpose," albeit concentrating on the larger vehicles Americans preferred. Its profits were monumental. But since the first oil shock in the late 1960s, that market share has steadily declined and incredibly, now sits at under 20 percent. As a result of this catastrophic market-share slump, GM experienced a financial collapse and eventually had to be rescued by the government. What led to this tragic downfall of an American industrial icon?

The outline of the story carries a familiar ring. As GM grew to prominence, it became bloated, bureaucratic, inward-looking, and complacent. Product quality slipped further year by year, causing long-lasting damage to the image of its brands. It became a sitting duck for a customer-focused competitor.

Enter Toyota, which had a perfect opportunity to make its move when oil prices spiked again in 1980. Essentially, Toyota pursued a three-pronged attack on a vulnerable GM. It:

▼ Introduced highly reliable, fuel-efficient cars, which consistently outperformed GM brands on product quality.

▼ Instituted the lowest manufacturing costs in the industry, based on the awesome Toyota Production System.

▼ Developed superior brand appeal, based on the total customer experience, exemplified by its Lexus brand.

While Toyota was the most successful, other Japanese competitors, such as Honda, followed a similar strategy, as GM's market share drained away bit by painful bit.

What was GM's reaction to this meltdown? Astonishingly, senior management repeatedly blamed the company's woes on its so-called heritage costs. During the good years it had agreed to generous worker benefits, such as pension and healthcare payments for retirees. These obligations eventually came to represent a cost penalty of about $2,500 per car, versus Toyota.

There is something I have never been able to understand about this explanation. Presumably, these heritage costs were fixed, rather than variable, costs. Therefore, as GM's market share continued to fall, the "heritage" cost penalty per car would inevitably rise, making this a largely self-inflicted wound. Let's assume that roughly half of the cost penalty ($1,250) was due solely to GM's market share collapse. This would mean that the $1,250 was actually a *value* deficit, not a cost deficit.

Another telling statistic is the estimate by James Womack, who heads up the Lean Enterprise Institute, that GM typically sold its cars, after discounts and cash rebates, at $2,000 less than the comparable Japanese models.[5] The statistic is revealing because it explains how GM's value deficit translates directly into dollars.

Now let's tally this up. If we add the $1,250 per-car value deficit arising from the market share loss to the cash discount gap of $2,000 per car, that puts GM's total value deficit at a jaw-dropping $3,250 behind Toyota on every car it sold.

It is not my purpose to take cheap shots at a company in dire circumstances. What I am interested in is the lessons we can learn from its difficulties. To begin with, it is pretty clear that GM's fundamental problem was only in part due to its cost disparity, important though that was. Its fatal "illness" was that it was losing out badly on value. How do we know that? Let's go back to our equation to assess competitive advantage. GM's problem lay in its crumbling numerator. Both its market share and auto prices suffered serious declines

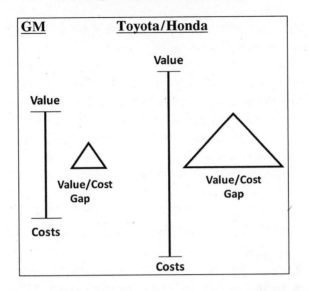

Figure 2.3   Toyota/Honda's Value/Cost Advantage versus GM's

versus Toyota and Honda. The Japanese car makers cleaned GM's clock at the value game. Toyota and Honda stretched the elastic band both at the top and the bottom to a much greater degree than GM was able to (see Figure 2.3).

With this persistent deficit on value, GM's fate was sealed. In recent years the company tried mightily to save its way to success, but this seldom works. Each time it experienced a negative step-change in volume, it moved to cut its costs to match the lower volume. By the time it had reached the lower cost level, volume had dropped even further, so it embarked on yet another round of cost cuts, in an endless chain reaction. With costs chasing volume downward, this amounted to a race to the bottom.

It's understandable that GM—and other organizations in similar situations—turn to cost-cutting as a strategy for salvation. Costs can be controlled internally; competitors cannot stop you. But lower costs represent a limited advantage. The competitor that beats you on value is the more serious long-term threat. Strategy is a bet on the future. Once you start to lose the value game, it's very difficult to scramble back, and your options for the future are severely limited.

To be fair, GM recently did make up impressive ground on quality. However, in products with a long purchase cycle, brand image is very "sticky," and in the end, product improvements came too late to save the company.

The key lesson here is that if you have a value problem, then that is what you must acknowledge and fix—and fast. You can't cure a value problem through cost reductions. It's like having liver disease and treating your lungs instead, and then expecting a cure. The only salvation for GM would have been an early diagnosis of the value issue and an urgent set of measures to turn around its brands. Failure to treat the right disease is what ultimately led to bankruptcy.

Value Leadership through a Winning Proposition

This brings me to a pet peeve. Over and over again, I hear organizations seeking to define their "value proposition." This always concerns me. Pursuing value is obviously the right thing to do, but this is plainly not a competitive statement. It ignores the most important question of all: How much value? In a competitive marketplace, absolutes have no meaning. It's the margin of difference—the gap—that counts. All value is relative, and customers have choices. Competitive advantage comes from providing *greater* value than your competitors for your chosen customers. The task, in other words, is *value leadership*.

This is where the words we use really matter. If something is crucially important, we should make it explicit, not hint at it indirectly. The problem is that companies so often allow the competition for superior value to be implicit, so that it happens by default. They need to make it explicit, and the way to do that is through a clear Winning Proposition.

An organization's Winning Proposition encapsulates measurable competitive advantage and defines how an organization will win the competition for value creation. It does that by answering these questions:

▼ What unique benefits will we offer our customers that will provide a compelling reason for them to choose us over our competitors?

▼ How will we translate this exceptional customer value into superior financial returns for our enterprise?

These two questions force you to define how to capture both superior customer value and superior economic value, and how to convert the one into the other.

The first question is a reminder that we must adopt an outside-in view of the world. An inside-out view will lead you to think you are selling products or services. But if you take an outside-in perspective, it becomes clear that customers are not buying products or services; they are actually buying benefits.

For example, when customers buy Windex, the window cleaner, the benefit they are seeking is not the product itself. They are seeking streak-free, clean windows. When they buy a lawn fertilizer, they want to create a beautiful lawn that will enhance their homes and be the envy of their neighbors. If these products fail to deliver on the benefits, the underlying businesses will fail. Many businesses make the mistake of defining themselves purely by the products they make—"We're in the fertilizer business." What they find hard to do is define the competitive benefits those products provide. Defining those benefits with clarity not only makes them more competitive, it clarifies to everyone inside the organization what they need to concentrate on, each and every day.

The second question is actually a zinger. If you don't have to generate superior profits, the first question becomes dead easy. You could just load your products with lavish benefits and sell them at half price! Customers would love that. Balancing the first and second questions is what makes business success so hard to achieve.

Note that this second question challenges a business to aim at *superior* financial returns. Why not just *satisfactory* returns? There are a few compelling reasons for this:

▼ Investors, just like customers, have choices. Superior returns enable you to raise capital more readily and at a cheaper cost than competitors.

▼ Competitors with higher gross margins can outspend you on R&D, advertising, and human development, to fuel their growth at your expense.

▼ Consistently superior financial results eventually raise the price/earnings ratio on your stock. A strong stock price can be used by you as currency for acquisitions. Conversely, a weak stock price can make you an easy acquisition target.

What's Your Winning Proposition?

The GM debacle underscores the need for every business to have a clear Winning Proposition that will define its competitive advantage and galvanize the energies of its people behind the right things. In order to lead an organization effectively, that Winning Proposition has to live in the hearts and minds of all the employees who are expected to act on it. Many executives seem to have difficulty nailing down a clear Winning Proposition, and too often will fudge this critical component of their strategy with some vague rambling statement that doesn't do the job. That's tantamount to an army marching into battle without a clear definition of how it will win, with the general saying, "Just go out there and fight. Execution is everything." That clearly is a cop-out for effective leadership.

The essential starting point for a Winning Proposition is to capture the simple essence of the benefits your organization will provide. Here are some examples:

Google: "We organize the world's information and make it universally accessible and useful."

Lego: "We offer products whose unique design helps children learn systematic, creative problem solving—a crucial twenty-first-century skill."

Institute for the Future: (a nonprofit research organization, of which I was once the chairman): "We are sense makers about alternative futures, to help organizations make better decisions in the present."

Hallmark Cards, Inc.: "We help people connect with one another and give voice to their feelings."

The key attribute of all these statements is that they focus on the superior benefits customers will receive, not just the internal actions these organizations will take. They offer a compelling reason why customers should choose to do business with them.

What's *not* a Winning Proposition?

Here's a statement that far too many organizations produce when I ask them for their Winning Propositions:

"We are the best in our industry at operational effectiveness."

My answer is, that's good, but it's not enough. You can be as efficient as you like, but if you don't have customers, you're broke. You must describe both your numerator (customer value) and your denominator (costs).

Another common response to my question:

"Our efforts are all directed at creating superior shareholder value."

Unfortunately, this statement is not useful. Shareholder value is an outcome (like the bottom line), not a strategy. It's like a coach telling a football team that they need to end the game with the highest score. We can assume they know that already. The question is *how*. Without creating superior value for customers, I doubt there is a business in the world that can generate superior shareholder value. Leaders need to define how an organization will generate that customer value. Shareholder value will surely ensue—provided, of course, it does that efficiently.

A Winning Proposition is, in short, the centerpiece of strategy. If an organization can't define its Winning Proposition in a simple and compelling way, it can't claim to have a strategy. The acid test of whether an organization has a Winning Proposition is whether the resulting actions achieve competitive advantage.

The Moment of Truth

Most of these lessons are encapsulated in the following story.

About seven years ago, a very large global company was scouring the world to find a business school to run a series of leadership programs for its top 400 executives. Columbia Business School (where I am a faculty member) ended up on the short list and I was asked by our Executive Education dean to lead our effort to win this business. This was going to be a very big deal indeed for the school. And, of course, it was a very important decision for this company.

The contest boiled down to two schools, and I was asked to fly to this company's headquarters for a final "showdown" meeting. There I was met by an extremely serious-looking committee, all dressed in dark business suits. The mood was somber. While the committee members were very courteous, nobody actually smiled. All eyes were scrutinizing me, and I felt a mild tension-sweat trickling down my back.

After a brief exchange of pleasantries, the chairman of the committee (let's call him Sam) asked me if I had brought a PowerPoint presentation. I eagerly said yes, and was about to leap up and get the show going. But Sam stopped me. "Before you show us your presentation" he said, "I have a question for you." I thought he was going to ask me something personal, such as where I lived or whether I owned a dog. But it was a business question: "Why should we choose to do business with Columbia?"

Oh, boy. Here was a real moment of truth. But I had gotten lucky. It so happened I had rehearsed my summation over and over, summarizing, simplifying, clarifying the essence. Now, instead of doing this at the end, I had to do it at the beginning. So I gave the two-minute speech.

My Winning Proposition was encapsulated in three points:

▼ This would not be a standard set of MBA lectures. The program would be highly customized to *your* needs, based on a deep analysis of the issues in *your* industry and how *you* achieve competitive advantage.

▼ We have an obligation to bring the very best ideas in the world, regardless of their origin.

▼ Our philosophy is that no matter how brilliant an idea may be it has absolutely no value until it is translated into action. Not only will we bring you the best ideas but we will always combine them with powerful and practical tools that enable you to act on them and measure their results.

Last, I promised that as the faculty director of the program, I would be personally responsible for these outcomes.

Nobody smiled. Sam then asked me to give my PowerPoint presentation. At the end of the meeting, we all shook hands, and off I went back to New York.

On the way to the airport, I called the dean, who asked how things had gone. I said, "I have no idea. Nobody smiled." The next day, the call came through: Columbia had been selected!

Nevertheless, Sam's question stuck in my mind: "Why should we choose Columbia?" He had put me on the spot, and rightly so. He knew that this was the most important question for any business to answer for the customers it wishes to serve. In my language, Sam was asking, "What is your Winning Proposition?"

Over the years of running executive programs for this company, I came to know Sam on a personal level. He had risen to the very top rungs of his organization. One day as we were chatting, I referred back to that meeting and that question he had asked. He also remembered it clearly. I asked him to tell me what would have happened if I had given him an unconvincing answer to his question. His reply summed it up beautifully and spoke on behalf of all customers everywhere: "I would have allowed you to continue with your PowerPoint presentation, but I wouldn't have listened to a word you were saying."

Applying Strategic Learning to Create an Adaptive Enterprise

3

Strategic Learning
Four Key Steps, One Cycle

It is not the strongest of the species that survives, nor the most intelligent, but the one most responsive to change.
—Charles Darwin

I n 1994, at age 33, Marco Pierre White became the youngest chef ever to be awarded three Michelin stars. The British chef and restaurateur of course had exceptional skills at the stove. But that's not the reason that the world's most demanding restaurant guide awarded him its ultimate accolade.

White, who has since retired, had to ensure that every activity and output of his restaurants, both in the kitchen and the dining room, was coordinated to produce excellence at the same high standards, meal after meal, without exception, to the demanding patrons who paid top prices for, and expected to be wowed by, a constant menu of creativity. To achieve and sustain these best practices while managing a pressure cooker of chaos and conflicting egos, White instilled a clear organizational process and applied it relentlessly. He was an extremely demanding taskmaster, and didn't tolerate any deviations that might compromise quality. His approach was based on a simple philosophy: *Complexity creates confusion, confusion creates inconsistency, and inconsistency creates failure.*[1]

White's claim to fame may rest on his palate, but his real achievement was turning creativity into a system that reliably replicated mouth-watering results on a daily basis for 17 years. That level of accomplishment doesn't require a charismatic superstar leader, nor is it limited to any field. Think of Wal-Mart's supply chain management, global design consultant IDEO's method for targeted brainstorming, or the ExxonMobil Safety Protocol, which, in the last three years has ensured that less than five tablespoons of oil were spilled per million gallons shipped by ExxonMobil's marine vessels.[2]

What these and other effective organizations have in common is that they know the secret for bridging the gap between doing something and excelling at it, which is an ingrained organizational process and continuous improvement through practice. What about your organization?

Do You Have a Robust Method?

I often ask the managers attending my executive seminars to take the test laid out on Figure 3.1, designed to analyze the strength of their organization's method of strategy creation. Based on their responses, I'd estimate that a majority of companies are living on the edge. Their planning methods are far more robust than their strategy methods.

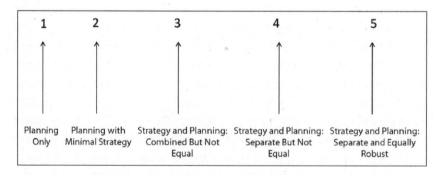

Figure 3.1   Strategy versus Planning Assessment

Generally speaking, an organization that considers itself poor at strategy has no effective method of producing it. If a company scores a 1, it does planning but has no strategy. Companies that rate 3 on the scale have a single process typically called "strategic planning," which is aimed at combining both a strategy and a plan in the same process. In those companies, the planning elements usually swamp the strategic elements, so there's no really robust strategic dialogue. It's more a matter of filling in a planning and budgeting form with some strategic elements in it—the ingredients for a toxic mixture.

Companies that move above a 3 have separate processes for each of strategy and planning. Those that rate themselves a 4 consider their planning process to be stronger than the strategy part—the processes are separate but not equal. If an organization makes it to a 5, it has separate and equally robust processes for both strategy and planning.

Are there companies that have reached this state of nirvana? There's a simple way to find out. When I work with a company, I ask to see its corporate calendar. I know it has deadlines for delivering corporate budgets, because every company needs to meet certain deadlines for reporting their financial results and prognostications. The test is when I say, "Show me the deadlines for your strategy discussions." If the response is, "We don't do it that way," then I know they don't have a method. When budget time comes around, you don't head off on vacation. It's the same with companies that are serious about strategy. They're rigorous about the process.

As mentioned before, strategic thinking starts with a method. Strategic functioning involves making decisions based on this method. Why is it necessary to have a systematic method? Because collective effort is clarified and mobilized through a systematic organizational process. Collective excellence is achieved through repetition, deliberate practice, and effective learning to continuously improve the desired outputs of such a process.

What Were We Thinking?

Why don't the most conventional methods of strategy work? It's not only that they're heavy on planning and light on strategy.

Fundamentally, they are static methods in a dynamic world: They fit a VUCA landscape about as well as a square peg in a round hole.

Before we redefine how to do strategy, it's instructive to figure out how the planning-intensive approach became so engrained in our thinking. In researching this topic, I discovered an answer that is both surprising and, I think, very important: that many existing methods of strategy derive from the school of scientific management promulgated by nineteenth-century efficiency expert Frederick Winslow Taylor and his French counterpart, Henri Fayol.[3]

Like Taylor, Fayol, a mining engineer, applied scientific method to the perennial problem of getting the most out of people, a problem sharpened during the second half of the nineteenth and first quarter of the twentieth century when national industries were growing out of local trades and small factories were expanding into enormous plants. These events and, later, the cataclysm of World War I, put a premium on efficient production.

Fayol's work provided the intellectual underpinnings of scientific management. He was the first person to define management: The role of management is to forecast and plan, to organize, and command, to coordinate, and control. Its object: to create order, cohesion, and predictability. Its tools: a militaristic command-and-control approach.[4]

What companies call strategic planning is often anchored in this thinking, and a number of companies are still shackled to these old ideas. What makes them not just old but outmoded is that their goal is to achieve an orderly, predictable state. For these companies, strategy is a numbers game rather than an ideas game—a planning ritual rather than a process of discovery. That's an appropriate goal in a stable environment but one completely unsuited as our environment has become much more dynamic. Focused on creating one-time, A-to-B change, this approach to strategy provides no means for generating *ongoing* adaptation. Such a practice could prove fatal today.

A number of efforts have been made to break free of these shackles, recognizing that this approach works for planning and budgeting but not for the strategic choices we need to make in a dynamic environment. I want to doff my hat to people like Michael Porter, who emphasized the point that strategy is all about competitive rivalry. His Five Forces model offers a basic analytical framework within which companies can develop an advantageous positioning to capture competitive advantage.[5] That was a big advance from Fayol's and Taylor's methodology; but in my opinion it didn't go quite far enough, because it, too, is a somewhat static method. Porter's Five Forces model is more of a snapshot of what is, rather than an understanding of dynamics or a process for continuous renewal.

We need a break from the past, not a modification or extension. While static models can help define a one-time change, we need to reinvent the role of strategy to help us adapt and thrive in a VUCA world.

Nature is our best teacher.

The Theory of Natural Selection

Peter Drucker wrote, "What is important is not the tools by themselves. It is the concepts behind them."

What, then, is the key concept behind a great strategy process?

In today's VUCA environment, the ability to create an adaptive enterprise is the *only* sustainable advantage. Thus, sustainable competitive advantage is not a product or a service. Those things have an ever-decreasing shelf life. Rather, it is an *organizational capability*. An adaptive enterprise is one with the built-in ability to renew itself over and over again, by sensing and rapidly responding to change on a continuous basis. This is important, because to win once is not enough: You must be able to *go on* winning.

That shouldn't be a surprise to anyone remotely familiar with Darwin's theory of natural selection.[6] In nature, the creation of favorable variations is the key to successful adaptation. Nature generates variations through a massive and ceaseless set of experiments, mutations that test a wide range of survival strategies. Most of these variations are failures. The variations that arise are generated without apparent design, and the ones that will survive are not predictable. As a result, evolution is a low-odds game: 99 percent of the species that ever existed are now extinct.

But a few succeed, enabling individual organisms to live longer, reproduce in greater numbers, and outcompete other species. These are the favorable variations that will come to dominate future generations.

As in nature, the rules of survival in the marketplace are essentially Darwinian. In nature, if you're unable to create favorable variations, you become extinct. That's the harsh rule of nature, and it's also the harsh rule of business. If you allow other organizations to create favorable variations—those that result in competitive advantage—and you sit still, you'll go out of business.

Nature's low odds are due to two gigantic learning disabilities: When nature fails, it doesn't know why; when it succeeds, it doesn't know why. People have one crucial advantage over other organisms: the power to think and learn. In the world of organizations, effective learning is at the heart of successful adaptation.

Darwin's theory of natural selection basically describes three steps that are the keys to successful adaptation: *variation, selection*, and *retention*. Translated into the marketplace:

1. *Variation* involves creative thinking, challenging assumptions, experimentation, and developing fresh insights.

2. *Selection* means identifying where to compete, how to win, and the key priorities for success.

3. *Retention* comes down to creating alignment within your organization and winning hearts and minds to support your strategy.

Now the challenge is to convert theory into a pragmatic process that breaks with the old static view of strategy creation and promotes continuous favorable variations through ongoing adaptation and renewal.

Two approaches in particular have held out the promise of improving an organization's ability to adapt: complexity theory and the notion of the learning organization. Neither on its own has worked.

Complexity Theory

The failure of traditional approaches to strategy sparked a growing interest in complexity theory as a way to think about adaptation and renewal. Borrowing concepts from biology and other natural sciences, the complexity theorists argue that in a nonlinear world, you cannot accurately predict the future, nor can companies plan ahead. Therefore, conditions should be created that allow strategy to emerge "naturally" and permit organizations to "self-organize" in response to signals from the external environment, as flocks of birds, for example, migrate successfully together, instinctively responding to environmental cues.

There are a number of valuable insights in complexity theory: the need to understand organizations holistically, the importance of allowing enough freedom for creativity to flourish, and the crucial role of organizational learning. However, human organizations are not flocks of birds, schools of fish or swarms of bees. People have free will. They can and do make choices that are often at odds with the goals of the organization. They can resist change, sabotage strategy and even go on strike. In other words, they don't always fly south in an orderly manner.

Learning Organizations

The central insight of the learning organization movement was encapsulated by Arie de Geus, formerly of Shell Oil and author of *The Living Company* (Harvard Business School Press, 1997), who observed, "In the future, an organization's ability to learn faster than its competitors may be its only sustainable competitive advantage."[7]

By emphasizing that learning is at the heart of adaptiveness, de Geus and others make a valuable contribution. Theirs is an important insight, but incomplete. It positions learning as an end in itself, rather than as a means to an end. It doesn't tell us clearly enough where to concentrate our scarce learning resources to achieve successful adaptation. Arguably, this is the most critical choice of all. If we try to learn everything, we will learn nothing.

Learning gives us half of the adaptation equation. To complete it, we must explicitly link learning to the creation and implementation of winning strategies. We need to add the dimension of *strategic focus*.

Strategy's New Mission

The key, then, is to focus our learning in the right way in order to shift from the original notion of strategy as planning to strategy as learning, and thus to the new mission of strategy: to create an adaptive enterprise. But in a way, we're back to square one: We need a *method* of doing strategy that enables us to adapt and renew in response to a shifting environment.

Every effective business process begins by defining its outputs. Work happens through processes that make it happen. Winning strategies will emerge only through a deliberate and practical process for generating insight, making choices, acting on them, and then adapting successfully as the environment changes. The outputs of a robust strategy method are what I call the "five killer competencies."

The Five Killer Competencies

I believe every organization must master the following critical skills to become an adaptive enterprise:

Insight: In a VUCA world, your organization needs the ability to make sense of the changing environment through powerful tools that generate superior insights into market trends, the evolving needs of customers, and the organization's own realities. This is where the competition begins. In fact, the competition for insight is the most decisive battle today.

Focus: Throughout the ages, no lasting success has been built without a robust process that translates superior insights into an intense focus on the right things. This involves the ability to make the most intelligent strategic choices about where you will compete, how you will win, and how you will prioritize your scarce resources in support of your Winning Proposition.

Alignment: Every element of your entire organization—measurement and reward systems, organizational structures and processes, your corporate culture, and the skills and motivation of your people—must be aligned and energized behind your strategic focus. This is a crucial leadership challenge, and without success here, no strategy can succeed.

Execution: A rigorous discipline for executing better and faster than competitors is essential. Speed in carrying out your strategy expands the gap between you and your nearest competitors and improves your ability to take advantage of the next shift in the environment—which is likely to happen sooner than anyone expects. But you'll be able to do this only when the first three competencies are in place.

Renewal: Finally, you'll need the ability to do these things repeatedly, thus creating a cycle of continuous learning and adaptation.

Note that the fifth competency is different from the first four. The first four competencies are aimed at producing specific outputs. The fifth creates an *ongoing cycle of renewal*. The ability to constantly renew your organization separates truly dynamic organizations from those that are doomed to become tomorrow's dinosaurs. It is the ultimate killer competency.

The Strategic Learning Cycle

Strategic Learning is a practical organizational process for mobilizing the five competencies to create an adaptive enterprise (Figure 3.2). Unlike traditional strategy, which aims at producing one-time change, Strategic Learning redefines the mission of strategy as creating the capacity to be adaptive through a built-in process for sensing and responding to change on a continuous basis.

The Strategic Learning process mobilizes the principles of evolutionary theory, which gives us the best explanation of how

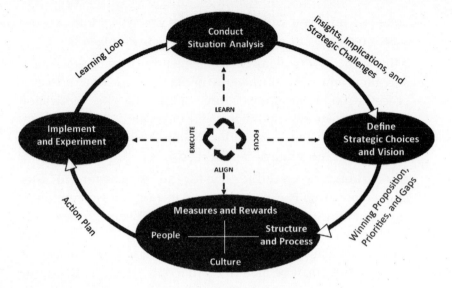

Figure 3.2 Leading through Strategic Learning

successful adaptation works. It's all about generating favorable variations—or, in the marketplace, Winning Propositions. Favorable variations are the ones that survive for a very simple reason: They have developed a competitive advantage in the competition for limited resources. The research is clear: If you smother your ability to sense and respond to changing conditions, if you stop adapting through the creation of favorable variations, you are doomed. It is true in nature and true in business.

What We've Learned from Deming

One of the key lessons quality guru W. Edwards Deming taught us about process excellence is that it's no good doing all of the things some of the time or some of the things all of the time. Process integrity means doing all of the things all of the time.[8]

When the outcome of a total process is defective, we frequently fall into the trap of blaming the last step. We'll say, "Oh, we're bad at execution." Deming was very good at pointing out that if the output wasn't satisfactory, the problem might not be with execution. It could be with any of the preceding steps. Execution doesn't have a life of its own. It's a derived capability; it results from what came before it.

This lesson is vitally important when applied to the Strategic Learning process. The process has four linked action steps—*learn, focus, align,* and *execute*—which build on one another. The first two steps form the basis of an organization's strategy creation. The third and fourth steps are the foundations of strategy implementation. Strategy creation and implementation are integrated in a mutually reinforcing process. The cycle is then repeated continuously—the fifth step—to embody the five competencies for sustainable competitive advantage.

One of my favorite African proverbs neatly encapsulates the chain of causation linking the steps in the Strategic Learning process: "Do not look where you fell, but where you slipped." When you're not satisfied with the outputs you're getting at a particular step in the cycle, look to the preceding step. If execution is not where you want it to be, check whether your alignment is well done. If alignment isn't working, look for what is clouding your clarity of focus. If you are unable to focus on the right strategic choices, maybe there's something wrong with the way you generated insights about the changing environment.

The single biggest concern I have had in working with organizations implementing the Strategic Learning process is when they just go through the motions. You won't find your Winning Proposition by playing with words. A process will deliver results that are only as strong as the weakest point in the chain of events. The quality of the outputs makes all the difference between doing Strategic Learning and excelling at it. The higher the quality of the output at each step, the higher the quality of the output at the next stage. You can make the process deliver excellence only by constantly improving the outputs at each step.

Building Capability through Deliberate Practice

As Aristotle explained, "Excellence is not an act but a habit. *We are what we repeatedly do.*"[9]

Provocative research by K. Anders Ericsson, a psychologist at Florida State University, has consistently and overwhelmingly shown that *experts are always made, not born.*[10] Superior performance is not so much an outgrowth of natural talent as of what Ericsson terms "deliberate practice," a considered, specific, and sustained effort to improve and excel at the skills you already possess and to extend the reach and range of your skills.

The essential difference between a top-ranked violinist at age 20 and one who is judged by conservatory teachers to be "only" second- or third-ranked comes down to hours of practice: 5,000 hours for a third-ranked performer, 7,500 hours for one in the second tier, and 10,000 hours—or 10 years—of practice for the Midoris and Joshua Bells of this world.[11] The same holds true for neurosurgeons, chess players, firefighters, actors, writers, computer programmers, airplane pilots, and many others. Even Winston Churchill, one of the most charismatic speakers of the twentieth century, routinely practiced his oratory style in front of a mirror.

Golfer Sam Snead, who holds the record for winning the most PGA Tour events, famously said, "Practice puts brains in your muscles."[12] But mindlessly hitting 10,000 golf balls or simply sawing away at the strings is not enough to achieve excellence. Deliberate practice entails constant assessment, feedback, analysis, and the ability to take what you have learned and apply it. It requires dedication and hard work. But the rewards are inevitable: Deliberate practice makes perfect.

The same holds true for leaders and organizations, and for any process in which you wish to excel. Just like any other core competency, Strategic Learning must be repeated over and over so it becomes ingrained. You are building capability through practice: strengthening key skills, developing new ones, identifying and eradicating faults, learning when and how to change behavior, articulating, and aiming for excellence.

Simply following the Strategic Learning process once is not enough. The leadership challenge is to repeat it over and over, so that an organization continuously learns from its own actions and from scanning the environment, and then modifies its strategies accordingly. The more often an organization repeats this cycle, the better it will become at doing it, thus enhancing its adaptive capacity. The result is a process of ongoing renewal that characterizes the truly adaptive organization.

We'll talk about how to excel at each of the steps in the cycle, and how to put them all together to ensure sustainable competitive advantage, in the next chapters.

Learn

Using a Situation Analysis to Generate Superior Insights about Your External Environment and Your Own Realities

The real voyage of discovery consists not in seeking new landscapes but in having new eyes.

—Marcel Proust

Why do businesses fail?

I noted in Chapter 1 that the rate of business failures is inexorably increasing. It's natural to assume that the main reason businesses fail is that they are unable to execute effectively. Right? In fact, wrong.

Business sage Peter Drucker summed up the reality. Most business failures, he said, are not the result of things being done poorly. Businesses fail most often because the assumptions on which the organization has been built and is being run no longer fit reality.

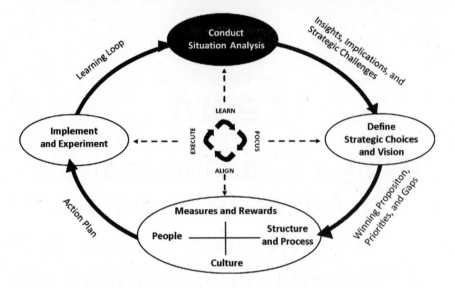

Figure 4.1 Leading through Strategic Learning: Learn

These assumptions, he said, involve markets, customers, competitors, and a company's own strengths and weaknesses.[1] McKinsey, the well-known management consulting firm, came to the same conclusion (*McKinsey Quarterly*, August, 2006). They stated bluntly: "Those who say that business success is all about execution are wrong."[2]

Their conclusion: Bad choices trump good execution every time.

The "Sense and Respond" Imperative

It is a condition for success that organizations must become "sense and respond" enterprises in order to go on adapting as the environment changes. Drucker's and McKinsey's point is that concentrating just on responding isn't good enough. You have to complete the sensing part of the formula first—and *excel* at it—if you want to produce the most intelligent response. The aim, after all, is to outsmart your competitors, not just participate in the game.

It is for this reason that the Strategic Learning process always starts with a Situation Analysis, a rigorous and systematic exercise for generating superior insights into the external environment and an organization's own realities (see Figure 4.1). The Situation Analysis is the engine room of strategy creation. Outperforming competitors on insights and then acting on them is what gives an organization its highest probability of success. This is where the competition for competitive advantage really begins. As the ancient Chinese military strategist Sun Tzu pointed out, a war is won or lost before the first battle is fought.[3]

The Situation Analysis is not the end in itself. It is the means to an end. The sole aim of the Situation Analysis is to develop superior insights as the basis for making the smartest choices about where you will compete and how you will win the competition for value creation. Those choices are encapsulated in your Winning Proposition, from which you will create your organization's Key Priorities and a plan to implement them.

Learning through the Situation Analysis

The task of the Situation Analysis is to generate superior insights into the following five key areas of inquiry:

▼ Customers and stakeholders
▼ Competitors
▼ Industry dynamics
▼ The broader environment
▼ The organization's own realities

For maximum benefit, the Situation Analysis should engage the intellectual and creative resources of the organization as widely as possible, not just those at the top. To achieve this, the approach I recommend is to assemble five cross-functional teams comprising four to six members each, one team for each of the five areas of inquiry. Each team should be led by a team captain. These five areas of inquiry represent a diverse set of "lenses," or perspectives, to ensure that all the crucial angles and possible connecting points are explored. In smaller organizations, two or three representatives for each area would suffice. The teams should have a balance of diversity and expertise. Diversity will bring fresh perspectives, but it is also necessary to have relevant experts represented on each team—for example, financial and HR experts on the Own Realities team, sales and marketing professionals on the Customer team, and so on.

Each team is given a set of Guiding Questions to pursue. Clearly, these Guiding Questions will vary somewhat, depending on the nature of the industry and whether the organization is for profit or not-for-profit. Each organization must find the right questions for its particular circumstances. The task of each team is to start off with these questions, which will in turn lead to further questions, and then to keep probing, sifting, and clarifying until the insights emerge.

The teams usually work for four to six weeks on the Situation Analysis, with team captains meeting regularly to compare notes, coordinate their work, and avoid duplication of effort.

The teams follow a process like the one shown in Figure 4.2.

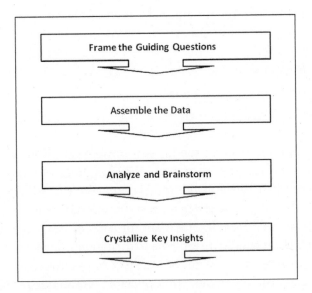

Figure 4.2   Situation Analysis Process

The method for doing a Situation Analysis is essentially Socratic. As Eugene Ionesco said, "It is not the answer that enlightens, but the question."[4] Great insights are invariably born from great questions. These are our "portals of discovery." Throughout the ages we have expanded the frontiers of knowledge not by resting on answers but through the relentless pursuit of questions. It is noteworthy that the first part of the word *question* is *quest*.

As the teams pursue their questions they should continue to dig and delve, and not stop this process of discovery until they have uncovered the most important underlying insights—those "brutal truths" they dare not walk away from. Seeing them first and understanding them better than competitors is the name of the game.

What follows is a list of sample questions for each area of inquiry.

Analyzing Customer Needs

How would the Customer team go about its work?

Let's look at the best way to tackle question 1 (Figure 4.3).

To prevent this task from becoming so overwhelming that you're paralyzed, I offer a technique that I have found always breaks the deadlock: When you ask a big question, such as "What are the trends in customer expectations," break it down into manageable pieces. Here's how this would work:

---

❶ What are the trends in customer expectations?
How is today different from yesterday?
How will tomorrow be different from today?

❷ What are useful ways to segment customers?
Which segments will we target? Which not?

❸ What is the hierarchy of needs of our targeted customers?
(i.e., What do they value most?)

❹ How well do we and competitors serve those needs today?
(S=Strong, M=Moderate, P=Poor)

Figure 4.3 Guiding Questions: Customers

1. First, look at what customer expectations are *today*. Define these expectations in simple, specific ways, not generalities.

2. Next, ask what customers expected *yesterday*, by which I mean over the past five years.

3. Then ask, how did yesterday become today? What were the drivers of that change? Was it competitor activity, a technological development, or some social norms that changed?

4. Find the "yesterday to today" story first and tell that story to each other. Challenge one another for clarity. Don't start thinking about tomorrow yet; at this point, it'll go nowhere.

5. Only *after* you have clarified and agreed on the story of how today emerged from yesterday should you pose the next question: How will tomorrow be different from today? What you're now doing is completing a story that you've already begun, instead of spinning a tale based on just gazing into the future.

As an example, let's consider the evolution of the business software industry. The story that might emerge from this exercise could run like this:

Yesterday, customer expectations were rooted in the ideas of Enterprise Resource Planning (ERP), which focused on an enterprise's internal operations. The emphasis was on improving efficiencies *within* functions, such as manufacturing and distribution. This was the era of efficiency with a small "e."

Today, these expectations are focused on supply chain management. This requires efficiency *between* functions—efficiency with a big "E." The functions needing to be integrated now extend outside corporate and national boundaries. Interoperability of software applications has become a key requirement.

Tomorrow will see the full realization of what has already begun—a world of "everywhere, all the time" access to the same body of information from any device, whether it be a desktop computer, a laptop, or mobile phone, plus the potential of buying software on demand, as if it were a utility.

Most of these changes have been driven by the twin factors of technology advancements combined with the forces of globalization.

The value of constructing a story such as this lies in the rich strategic dialogue it promotes. Trends tell the story. Snapshots never do. Science fiction writer William Gibson said, "The future is already here. It's just not evenly distributed yet."[5] All the signs and signals of what the future will bring are all around us. The task for us is not to try to predict the future, but to think imaginatively about the future consequences of today's realities.

As a team, you now understand something pretty significant and can proceed to question 2: What are useful ways to segment customers? Not all customers want the same thing. The point of this question is to help you group your customers according to their different expectations.

Staying with the business software example, one useful way to segment customers would be by industry sector; for example, banking, retailing, energy, automotive, aviation, and so on. While these customer groups share a set of common needs, each of them will also have its own distinctive requirements based on its type of business.

Questions 1 and 2 enable you to decide which customers you will aim to serve, and which not.

Now you are ready to tackle question 3. How can you find out what your targeted customers value most? This is a crucial question. It is impossible to create superior value for your customers unless you understand what they value most. The creation of your Winning Proposition is dependent on the answer to this question.

Wouldn't it be nice if we could simply ask customers what they value most? The trouble, of course, is that most customers are unable to articulate their needs in any coherent way. As Henry Ford famously said, "If I had asked people what they wanted, they would have said 'faster horses.'"[6]

Fortunately, there's another option.

We can find a good framework for exploring this issue by looking to Maslow's hierarchy of needs. Proposed by psychologist Abraham Maslow in 1943, it is often depicted as a pyramid

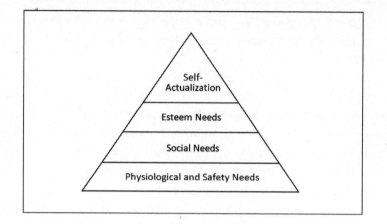

Figure 4.4   Maslow's Hierarchy of Human Needs

consisting of four levels, ranging from physiological and safety needs to social needs to esteem needs and, finally, to self-actualization needs, particularly those related to identity and purpose (see Figure 4.4).[7]

Each of the lower-level needs—what Maslow called "deficiency needs"—must be satisfied for an individual to be able to focus on the next level.

Now let's translate Maslow's hierarchy of human needs into a corresponding hierarchy of customer needs, as shown in Figure 4.5.

At the bottom of the pyramid are the basics, the "table stakes," that every organization is expected to provide to its customers just to stay in the game. Without table stakes, you can't play. However, table stakes, while necessary to survive, are not sufficient to thrive. To create greater value than your competitors and *excel* at delighting your customers, you have to move up in the hierarchy of customer needs.

An example of this is the competition between the so-called Big Four global accounting firms: Deloitte, KPMG, PWC, and E&Y. From a branding perspective, these firms tend to be seen by potential clients as a collective, rather than each having unique auditing skills. Auditing is a legally mandated activity with strict standards and rules, and generally speaking every member of the Big Four is trusted to provide a first-class audit.

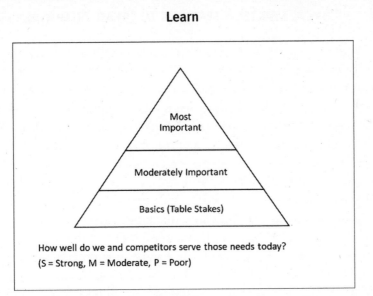

Figure 4.5 Customer Hierarchy of Needs

So how does a member of the Big Four develop a Winning Proposition? In other words, how does it break out of the pack by consistently delivering greater value to its clients than its competitors?

At first sight, one would be inclined to argue that winning in the audit game is all about doing the best audit, period. After all, look what happened to Arthur Andersen in the wake of the Enron scandal. Andersen's perceived auditing failure caused the collapse and disappearance of the firm.

But let's think again. If we look at this catastrophic event in the light of Maslow's hierarchy, we can see that Andersen actually failed because it failed to deliver the table stakes: a reliable audit. That's what knocked the firm out of the game. The point is that table stakes are not easy. They are professionally very demanding for an audit company. But looked at through the eyes of the client, they are not enough. Once those needs have been satisfied, clients expect more. This was exactly the Maslow argument. If you don't have food, shelter, oxygen (the bottom of the pyramid), then that's all you will think about. But if you do have those basics, your needs will shift to the next level in the hierarchy. The one is not a substitute for the other. These are building blocks.

What a member of the Big Four such as Deloitte understands is that it can't win by only doing a better audit. This is necessary, but not sufficient. With auditing excellence as its building block, Deloitte has been diligently researching what clients value beyond the table stakes, and developing those capabilities throughout the firm. These are benefits such as industry expertise, understanding of the client's economic engine and strategic challenges, assembling the right team, and providing seamless global service. Providing this total package is what the firm defines as the "Deloitte client experience."

Ericsson, the global telecommunications giant, is another good example. Although Ericsson has moved increasingly into services, its core business through the years has been supplying state-of-the-art network infrastructure for its customers, telephone operators such as AT&T, Verizon, and Vodafone. Engineering excellence is deeply embedded in the company's DNA, and it has a towering reputation for providing outstanding engineering solutions for its customers. However, Ericsson, just like Deloitte, has realized that in a world of intense global competition, unsurpassed engineering is what its customers now expect as an indispensable starting point. Customers are looking for value beyond those essential foundations.

The hierarchy of needs analysis has shown Ericsson that, in addition to outstanding engineering, customers place a high value on thought leadership about the future direction of the industry, rapid responsiveness, and creative solutions that enable operators to generate and retain customers. (Customer "churn" is a big problem for operators.) Ericsson has learned that it's an "and" game—state-of-the-art engineering *and* innovative multimedia solutions.

After analyzing your customers' hierarchy of needs, use a simple rating scale (strong, moderate, or poor) to determine how well your company meets those needs today versus key competitors. This comparative mapping will help you assess your value gaps and what it will take to win the competition for value creation in your game.

Excelling at Understanding Customers

One of the most frequent laments I hear is, "We are just not good at understanding customer needs. How can we get better at this?"

Of course, the mastery of techniques, such as the hierarchy of needs analysis, is a great help. Analytical frameworks help guide and clarify our thinking, as do well-constructed brainstorming sessions, focus groups, and so on. Improving these skills through deliberate practice will lead to better and better results.

That said, I believe that using this array of techniques is not nearly enough. There is another requirement—an emotional, not analytical, one—that might surprise you. You have to love your customer. I don't mean romantic love. I mean the kind of empathetic connection that enables you to truly understand the deeper needs and unspoken concerns of your customers.

Deborah Adler is a very talented graphic designer, who has created a groundbreaking new design for prescription drug bottles called Clear Rx. How that happened stems directly from her love for her grandmother.

While Deborah was still a student doing research for her master's degree at the School of Visual Arts, New York, her grandmother, Helen, mentioned a disturbing event. Helen had mistaken her husband's medication—the same drug but at a different dosage—for her own and swallowed it.

When Deborah looked in her grandmother's medicine cabinet, the source of the mistake was obvious. The packaging was practically identical, with the only difference being the dosage strength and her grandparents' first names—and even those began with the same two letters, H-E, for Helen and Herman. Furthermore, the text was so minuscule as to be practically illegible.

As Deborah began to delve into the problem, she recalls, "I was shocked to learn that 60 percent of Americans don't take their medication correctly. The number of prescriptions filled in the U.S. each year equals more than 10 per person. If you multiply that by the U.S. population, roughly 300 million, you're left with a staggering 3 billion prescriptions a year. That's a lot of room for medication mishaps."

Deborah moved into action mode and worked feverishly on a better design with clearer labeling. After numerous iterations and many late nights, she completed her breakthrough design. This included features such as color-coded neck rings for different members of the

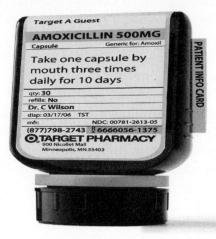

Figure 4.6 Clear Rx Prescription Bottle Design

family, and much better layout of the essential instructions and warnings (Figure 4.6). It was, literally, a transformation.

What Deborah needed next was a distribution channel. After months of determined effort, she found it through the Target retail chain's pharmacy departments. Her Clear Rx system has received awards ranging from the Good Housekeeping Institute to the Institute for Safe Medicine Practices, and was even featured in an exhibition at the Museum of Modern Art in New York. The publicity it has received put Target's pharmacy services on the map and stands to be a significant boost to the retailer's bottom line.

Having read about this design breakthrough, I invited Deborah to give a talk at a seminar for Ericsson executives. In the Q&A, everyone wanted to know how she became so good at design. I felt we were somehow missing the point, so I asked her the question that was preying on my mind: "I don't mean to be undiplomatic, but tell us honestly, how many designers do you think there are in the U.S. who are just as good as you are?" She smiled disarmingly and blurted out, "Oh, hundreds and hundreds!" "So then, tell us," I continued, "what's different about you?" She grew serious and replied, "You know, I really love my grandmother."

It was then that the Ericsson executives realized what Deborah's story had really taught them. If you genuinely care about your customers, the insights will come. And if you don't, well, forget it. Deborah's breakthrough flowed from her empathetic understanding of what customers like her grandmother valued most. The design was simply the creative means of providing that benefit. And, of course, she showed great determination in finding a pharmacy chain to adopt her design. But that passion came from the same source—she really loves her grandmother.

Let's move to the next area of inquiry, Key Stakeholders (Figure 4.7).

Who Are Our Stakeholders and Why Do They Matter?

The basic purpose of a business is to generate and retain customers. By doing so at a profit, we will create value for our shareholders. And achieving these things requires the support and commitment of our employees.

These are the three main stakeholders we usually think about: customers, employees, and shareholders. But in today's interconnected world, it has become increasingly important to create value for certain stakeholders beyond these three traditional ones.

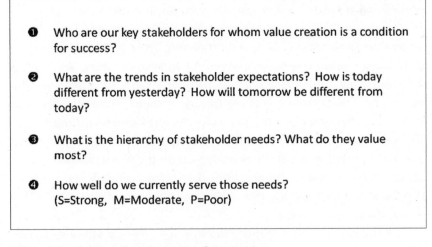

❶   Who are our key stakeholders for whom value creation is a condition for success?

❷   What are the trends in stakeholder expectations? How is today different from yesterday? How will tomorrow be different from today?

❸   What is the hierarchy of stakeholder needs? What do they value most?

❹   How well do we currently serve those needs? (S=Strong, M=Moderate, P=Poor)

Figure 4.7   Guiding Questions: Key Stakeholders

These additional stakeholders are those entities for whom we have to create value as a condition for our own success. These will vary by industry. We need to be explicit in identifying who these key stakeholders are, understanding their needs, and determining how to create superior value for them. In a sense, we have to treat these stakeholders as indirect customers. They may not be paying us money, but if we do not create value for them, we cannot achieve superior profits. The first of the Guiding Questions is the threshold question of identifying who these key stakeholders are for your organization. Thereafter, the questions are the same as you would use for customers.

As an example, let's look at the oil industry. Stripped down to its essentials, the challenge is to find, produce, and sell oil and petroleum products in the safest, most efficient, and profitable way. Revenue is generated only when these products are sold to customers. Everything up to that point essentially represents costs.

But the challenges facing the international oil companies (IOCs) mean they must generate superior value for stakeholders beyond the customers who buy their oil. Contrary to popular belief, the IOCs do not dominate this market. The real global giants are mainly the national oil companies (NOCs) owned by countries such as China, India, Venezuela, and Brazil, which are increasingly being motivated by resource nationalism (the drive to secure oil supplies as a matter of national security) rather than by pure profit considerations.

Among the key stakeholders in this high-stakes game are the resource owners, often foreign governments. The oil resources may be in Brazilian waters or under the soil of Nigeria or Chad. When all is said and done, competing successfully for *access* becomes the critical factor. The resource owners (many of them politically and economically unstable) are flexing their muscles more and more, and the NOCs are jockeying for advantage. In this context, an important success factor for the IOCs is understanding the needs and expectations of these stakeholders better than their competitors, bringing the best technology to the table, and developing a fair value exchange based on this.

Changes in the healthcare industry are creating similar imperatives for creating stakeholder value. The traditional business model for pharmaceutical or medical-device manufacturers was to develop superior solutions for patients, and then market these treatments to the doctors or surgeons. This approach is becoming outdated. Going forward, the patients and physicians will of course remain central, but they will no longer be the sole decision makers. Escalating costs have made this model unsustainable, and looming healthcare reform will strengthen the role of other major stakeholders.

In the future, drug and device manufacturers will have to create superior value, not for one or two discrete entities, but for a web of interdependent stakeholders that comprise the healthcare *system*.

▼ First are the patients; although they don't buy the treatments directly, they have much greater access to information through the Internet, are much more aware of their choices, and are demanding to be heard.

▼ Second are the doctors and surgeons, who seek the best alternatives for their patients.

▼ Third are the hospitals, which are under strong pressure to reduce costs and do things more efficiently.

▼ Finally, there are the insurance companies, which, as payers, are becoming key decision makers on what to pay for and where to place the limits.

Complicating this new healthcare marketplace is the fact that these stakeholders will often have conflicting aims. But for the manufacturers, offering benefits to one stakeholder at the expense of another stakeholder won't work. The key for them will be to have a deep understanding of the interlocking system of stakeholders, and the development of optimal solutions for that integrated system.

The competitive game is changing in every industry. Stakeholders beyond customers, employees, and shareholders are becoming more influential. It is important for every company to conduct a stakeholder analysis to identify the stakeholders for whom value creation is a condition for their own success.

Society as the Ultimate Stakeholder

The issue of social responsibility has been given much attention of late. There has been a lot of debate about the trade-off between profit and social responsibility—between doing well and doing good. Interestingly, employees are becoming more vocal on the issue. They want to feel that their companies have a social conscience. One result has been the growing number of organizations that have developed policy statements on social responsibility.

The era of transparency we now live in has brought this issue to the forefront. The world is a real-time witness and judge to everything companies do and do not do. Society at large has also found a voice in the form of the increasing number of influential NGOs that have embraced various causes, ranging from human rights to environmental safety. A few are strident and extreme, but their messages are nevertheless getting attention. Some will say that NGOs are not stakeholders because they have no "skin" in the game. It is true that they are not stakeholders in that sense. But they are a voice, no matter how imperfect, of the ultimate stakeholder: society as a whole.

The days of binary thinking are over, of seeing shareholders and society engaged in some sort of zero-sum game. The simple credo that shareholder value trumps all is no longer supportable, nor indeed will it serve shareholders in the longer term. Business is part of society, not distinct from it; and if it causes society harm, it cannot expect to prosper.

None of this throws up easy answers, but it does help us frame the right questions about the role and responsibilities of a business in society, and that debate is an important one. Above all, it places a responsibility on companies to be good listeners—listening with the intent to understand. Yes, listening to a preachy NGO argue that business is inherently evil can be galling, so good listening is sometimes hard to do. A useful foundation for this dialogue, therefore, is for the two sides to acknowledge their different starting points. NGOs come to the table with a social mission, whereas businesses inescapably have a commercial mission. The mistake is to view the two as mutually exclusive.

In the final analysis, this becomes a question of values. Ask yourself this question: As a company, what do you care about beyond just making money?

We move now to the Guiding Questions for Competitors (Figure 4.8).

Analyzing Competitors

Too often we overlook the vital importance of good competitor analysis. To paraphrase Sun Tzu again: If your enemy understands you better than you understand your enemy, you are sure to lose.[8] Recall that you must "mind the gap." Do you have a bigger value/cost gap than your competitors? In a competitive world, everything is comparative.

When asked about their knowledge of their competitors and how they operate, too many companies lapse into survey mode. You know the drill: Our main competitor is Company A; it operates in 55 countries, has 17 factories, and 15,000 employees; its revenue is $10 billion and its total return on investment is 20 percent. These are interesting statistics, but not very helpful. You really want to know how Company A is competing for the customers you're competing for. Hence the first question: In what distinctive ways are your competitors serving the market and needs of customers?

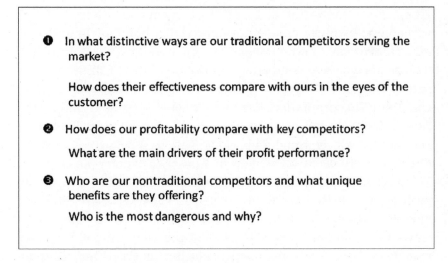

❶ In what distinctive ways are our traditional competitors serving the market?

How does their effectiveness compare with ours in the eyes of the customer?

❷ How does our profitability compare with key competitors?

What are the main drivers of their profit performance?

❸ Who are our nontraditional competitors and what unique benefits are they offering?

Who is the most dangerous and why?

Figure 4.8   Guiding Questions: Competitors

This question must be pursued through the eyes of the customer, not through your eyes. We tend to have a distorted view of our competitors. They are either fire-breathing dragons or misguided incompetents. Find out from your customers through dialogue and independent research how they perceive the distinctive value your competitors are delivering. Then consider how this value compares with the customer value you are delivering. Compare your findings with what the Customer group discovered about where competitors rank in the hierarchy of needs analysis.

Question 2: How does the profitability of key competitors compare with yours? What explains their profit performance?

I often run into people who complain, "I can't compare the profitability of my competitor's product line to mine because this specific information about them is hidden in a jungle of other businesses." It's true that companies are not legally required to disaggregate their profitability in detail in their published financial statements. No doubt your competitors would prefer that you don't know this. But that doesn't mean you can't get a reliable answer through smart analysis and good, old-fashioned savvy.

When I was the president of Tropicana, I was fortunate to have the expertise of Steve Shechtman, a senior planning executive in our group. Steve was one of the best I've seen at competitor analysis. He was able to estimate competitor profitability brand by brand or by individual product line and then track the trends. At the time, one of the brands we were competing against was Citrus Hill, which was part of Procter & Gamble. We wanted to know not just how profitable the P&G corporation was (which could be seen from its published accounts), but how much money P&G made from Citrus Hill, and then follow the trend. This would help us assess the size of the threat we were facing and to consider possible countermoves.

Steve approached the task like a puzzle, which he put together piece by piece. By looking at Citrus Hill's market share from our market research, he derived the revenue number. He then interviewed our operations people and put together a picture of their manufacturing system plus their packaging and distribution costs. From our salespeople he got an estimate of Citrus Hill's promotional expenditure, and from published sources he was able to pin down their advertising spending. From all this, Steve produced an estimate of the brand's profit statement. Each year, he would refine his estimate and map out the unfolding trend.

Steve's analysis showed that Citrus Hill was losing substantial money, but there was no way of proving the accuracy of these numbers. I said, "Steve, I'm not sure I believe these numbers. P&G is not irrational. Why would they continue with a loss-maker like this?" Steve bided his time and the next year announced that they were losing money again. "Mark my words," Steve said, "they will withdraw from this market. Citrus Hill is a dog in their portfolio. No sensible company would continue with it."

Sure enough, in due course, I read in the *Wall Street Journal* that P&G was closing down its Citrus Hill business. Meanwhile, based on Steve's assertions that P&G was losing money on Citrus Hill, we had tailored our competitive strategy to maintain just enough pressure on them, rather than spending heavily to combat them.

Soon after P&G's decision, we hired a former Citrus Hill brand manager. I asked him to look at Steve's profit assessment. As Citrus Hill was no longer in business, this was fair game. "Where did you get this?" he asked suspiciously. I explained, and then said, "Now, answer one question: Was this assessment within 10 percent of being accurate?" "No," he replied. "It's more accurate than that."

Knowing the profitability of your competitors—not just as a total company but the line of business that competes with your line of business—is an essential part of your Situation Analysis. Even though competitors don't disaggregate that information in their public accounts, you can do this. It's a question of honing the methodology. The answers you get will enable you to make even smarter strategic choices.

Question 3 gets at the issue of identifying who your indirect competitors are. We are prone to view our competitive set too narrowly. For example, cereals compete against bagels for "share of stomach" at breakfast time, and bagel consumption grew dramatically a few years ago. This was something Kellogg had to confront and contend with eventually, with entries such as Pop-Tarts and the like. Newspapers are not so much competing against other newspapers anymore; bloggers and other Internet news sources are becoming the main threat to their continued existence.

We're seeing more and more competitive convergence, and the old, fixed boundaries between industries are dissolving. Let's consider this list: television, telephones, computers, media, and entertainment. How many industries are on this list? If you are Sony, Ericsson, or Microsoft, you dare not view them separately. All these "industries" are interacting with each other in a complex, interdependent way, and each is a competitive threat to the others.

Let's look next at the Guiding Questions for Industry Dynamics (Figure 4.9).

Interpreting Industry Dynamics

Every industry is in a state of flux. Some changes amount to gradual revolutions, while other shifts are more sudden. No industry is static. Sometimes the surface seems calm, but beneath the surface various currents are swirling and changing the very structure of the industry. These dynamics bring threats and opportunities, for both you and your competitors. Over time they alter the rules of success. The former CEO of Ericsson, Carl-Henric Svanberg, regularly

---

❶ Which trends are most important in shaping the structure of our industry?

   What are their root causes and ultimate consequences?

❷ How are these trends changing the rules of success?

❸ What threats do these trends present to our profitability and business model?

   What opportunities do they open up?

Figure 4.9 Guiding Questions: Industry Dynamics

reminded his employees, "What brought us to the present will not carry us to the future."

The Guiding Questions focus on finding and interpreting the key trends in your industry, and clarifying their implications for choice-making.

In Chapter 1, I talked about Boeing's bet on the 787 Dreamliner, compared with Airbus's investment in the A380. These momentous decisions, which will carry consequences far into the future, were based essentially on different views of the future direction of the industry. Would the trends favor the point-to-point model (Boeing's bet) or the hub-and-spoke model (Airbus's bet)?

No doubt, both companies carefully analyzed the key trends in commercial aviation. This meant examining what passengers were looking for, what airlines were looking for, the needs and expectations of airports, the volume trends in domestic versus international travel, and so on. Each company had to establish an analytical framework for defining the key industry sectors and how these were evolving in terms of both volume and profitability. Based on this industry analysis, they had to make a diagnosis of where the most attractive opportunities lie, and make their choices accordingly. Who was right—or more right—Boeing or Airbus? Time will tell. This example illustrates that when you make choices, you are placing a bet on the future, not the past. Understanding the structure and trends within your industry is critical if you aim to outsmart your competitors.

Not every company is faced with making such once-in-a-decade, bone-crunching choices. Most businesses have to make a series of sometimes large and sometimes smaller choices every day that collectively must add up to a coherent direction. But that totality of choices is equally momentous. We need to apply the same rigor as did Boeing and Airbus in making their single big decision.

In my years at Tropicana, we were constantly tested by how well we were able to interpret industry trends and determine which market sectors would prove to be the most attractive. At that time, the "great divide" was between not-from concentrate (NFC) and from-concentrate (FC) orange juice. NFC juice required a much larger investment in assets and was much more expensive to produce and store, but was fresher-tasting and could command a premium price if successfully marketed. FC juice lent itself more to a lower price positioning. The Tropicana brand had to stand for something. Straddling the two sectors would blur our brand focus. Our analysis of trends told us that the brightest prospects lay with NFC. Our biggest competitor, Minute Maid, owned by Coca-Cola, opted to place its emphasis on FC juice. In the years that followed, Tropicana surged ahead in market share and profitability. The NFC bet turned out to be a good one.

Tropicana has since been bought by Pepsi, and the orange juice wars endure, as Pepsi continues to battle it out against Coca-Cola's Minute Maid.

The next area of inquiry is the broader environment (Figure 4.10).

Taking a Broader View

Analyzing industry dynamics involves looking at your particular industry. Analyzing the broader environment means looking at the overarching trends that cut across industries. The impact of these forces will vary by industry, so each organization must decide where

What's happening around us that will impact our business in regard to:

❶ Economic trends

❷ Social habits and attitudes

❸ Globalization

❹ Technology

❺ Demographics

❻ Government intervention

Figure 4.10   Guiding Questions: The Broader Environment

to deepen its inquiry. I have found that the topics listed in Figure 4.10 serve as a useful checklist.

What's an example of a key economic trend? Consider the huge shift in purchasing power from the old triad of North America, Western Europe, and Japan to Asia. More than 50 percent of the world's future economic growth is expected to be generated by China, India, and other Asian nations (not including Japan). If your firm depends entirely on its existing business in North America, Western Europe, and Japan, your share of the global market is already inexorably in decline. That is one consequence. The other is that aggressive new global competitors are emerging from these Asian economies, thereby increasing competitive intensity and putting added pressure on margins. China Mobile, for example, is already the world's largest telephone operator.

In the field of technology, the Internet is changing how the game is played in every industry and company I know. Power is shifting from sellers to buyers; supply chains are spanning corporate and national boundaries; transparency and knowledge-sharing have been dramatically enhanced; new sales and distribution channels are emerging; and everything happens faster.

Finally, the pendulum seems to be shifting to more government intervention in a wide number of sectors, including financial services, energy, food manufacturing, and healthcare. Whether this will be a long-term trend remains to be seen, but there is little doubt that greater regulation will have profound consequences for the industries affected.

So far, all the areas of inquiry have focused on the external environment, each bringing a different angle to the Situation Analysis. The final area of inquiry examines the organization's internal realities. Let's review the Guiding Questions, listed in Figure 4.11.

Facing Your Own Realities

Question 1 requires some critical thinking to begin with. What are your *critical* performance measures? To measure everything is to measure nothing. Every business has a handful of key indicators that will show how it is really doing—somewhere between five and

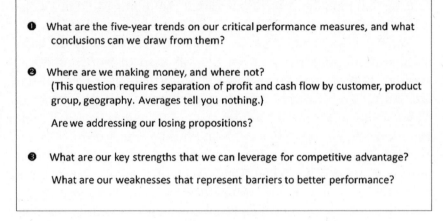

①   What are the five-year trends on our critical performance measures, and what conclusions can we draw from them?

②   Where are we making money, and where not?
(This question requires separation of profit and cash flow by customer, product group, geography. Averages tell you nothing.)

Are we addressing our losing propositions?

③   What are our key strengths that we can leverage for competitive advantage?

What are our weaknesses that represent barriers to better performance?

Figure 4.11   Guiding Questions: Own Realities

seven items. Beyond that, you are getting into the weeds. I grew up in the consumer products business. For this type of business, my view is that there are really five key indicators of underlying health: market share, gross margin percentage, return on sales, return on assets, and cash flow. If these five measures are healthy and growing over time, you know you have a healthy business.

Once you have identified the critical measures for your business, the next important task is to examine the trends. Many businesses just look at current results compared with budget or the same period in the prior year. This is a snapshot that will tell you very little. The only way to truly understand your business and diagnose the key issues is to dig into the trends. My rule of thumb is to look at five years. Trends will always contain a story. The objective is to find that story.

Question 2 requires disaggregation of your performance by product, customer segment, geography, and so on. The trouble with most financial reports is that everything is aggregated into a total result. This gives you an average. Averages have only one role in life: to hide the truth. And you can't manage an average; you can only manage the individual elements. Mark Twain summed up this dilemma with a humorous remark: "I have one foot in a bucket of ice and the other in a bucket of hot water, but on average I'm comfortable."

Portfolio Profitability Map

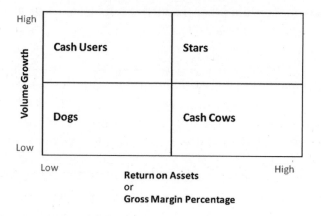

Figure 4.12   Disaggregation Map

A really useful technique to accomplish the task of disaggregation is the Portfolio Profitability Map, a matrix that segregates the profitability of the different parts of your business. Shown in Figure 4.12, it is a simplified version of the matrix originally conceived by the Boston Consulting Group.

For each part of the business you are measuring, the vertical axis looks at volume growth, and the horizontal axis examines either return on assets (ROA) if you are a product company, or gross margin percentage if you are a services company.

Assuming you are a manufacturing company, this is how it works: Those products that fall into the upper left quadrant (i.e., high-volume growth but low ROA) are typically "cash users." Your challenge will be to move these products over into the top right quadrant, which would convert them into the "stars" in your portfolio. Because of product life-cycles, stars almost always end up in the bottom right box, where they serve as useful "cash cows" in their mature years. The aim is to generate a cycle of renewal by using the cash cows to replenish the top left quadrant and then shift those new entries into the stars box, and so on.

What invariably occurs in a business is the development of an embarrassingly long list of underperforming products in the bottom left corner, popularly known as "dogs." Think of dogs as something like the junk most people accumulate in their attics—except that dogs waste money and other resources, not just storage space.

The purpose of disaggregation is to help you make the most intelligent choices based on your analysis of where you are making money and where you are underperforming. For products that are stuck in the dog box, there are only three options: close, fix, or sell these product lines. Allowing them to languish in the dog box dilutes everything else you are doing. Getting rid of them unleashes the power of focus. Product clutter is a huge drain on your resources.

Obviously, this analysis requires the allocation of shared costs according to a sensible allocation method. This is not hard to do. It may not be 100 percent accurate, but then absolute precision is not the aim. Ask yourself whether your conclusions would be any different if your cost allocations were off by 10 or 20 percent. Most often, the really important findings are right by a mile.

I serve as a coach to a family business in South Africa, called E. Snell & Co., the third largest company in South Africa's distilled spirits market, offering a wide product range of brandies, whiskies, vodkas, and so on. The two top players are large corporations with heavy clout and big advertising budgets, which forced Snells into a low-price mode, to protect its volume. Iain Hooper, the CEO, described his company's challenge as "dancing between the dragon's teeth." The result was that Snells was working with very narrow profit margins. Iain, together with the chairman (Iain's uncle, David Hooper), decided the time had come to address the profitability issue. They couldn't possibly outspend the big boys. They had to find a smart way to upgrade their margins.

At a strategy workshop with the executive team, we set about the portfolio profitability analysis. The results were extremely revealing. A small set of key brands was generating the bulk of the profit. Many of the secondary brands were nothing more than a drain on performance. Based on this exercise, Snells has embarked on a new strategy of brand focus, gradually increasing the emphasis on the high-margin brands and phasing out the losers. This did not require any big new investments. Rather, it was an investment in focus. Snells is now on the path to push up its margins inch by inch. Because the whole of the executive team was involved in the workshop, they are all committed to making the new strategy a success.

Question 3 is an examination of your organization's strengths and weaknesses. This is aided by the answers to the first two questions, but should go on to evaluate where you stand on factors such as competencies, reputation, scale, efficiencies, safety, culture, and so on.

Pulling Together the Situation Analysis

I recommend that the five Situation Analysis teams work on their respective areas of inquiry over a period of four to six weeks. They then get together to review the insights of each team, and pull together one integrated summary of the insights and their implications (Figure 4.13). These insights and their implications then become the essential input for making the strategic choices:

▼ Where will we compete?

▼ How will we win?

The Difference between Insights and Information

The key deliverable of the Situation Analysis is a set of penetrating insights, not mere information. What is the essential difference between the two?

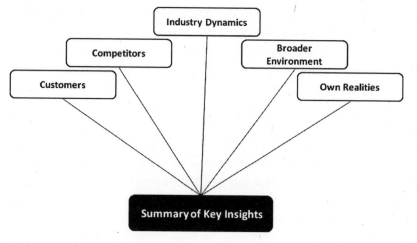

Figure 4.13 Learning through the Situation Analysis

To answer this question, think of gold mining.[9] To start with, you dig up something like four tons of gold ore. The ore has very little value until you refine it into one ounce of pure gold. The raw ore is the equivalent of information; the ounce of gold is the insight. That's where the real value lies. A Situation Analysis is exactly like extracting gold from ore. You start with a lot of information. After filtering, refining, analyzing, and synthesizing, you are able to extract a simple set of insights that help you outsmart your competitors.

Insights involve looking at a body of information and seeing the underlying truth. If "sight" is defined as "looking at," and "insight" means "seeing into," then what I am talking about is the art of seeing deeply. The value of an insight is that it explains things in ways that information cannot do. It enables you to see something in a new way.

The difference between insights and information is what separates a Situation Analysis from conventional surveys and polls. Those produce reams of information, but rarely useful insights.

Frequently, when I start to work with companies, they'll say, "We've already done a Situation Analysis." Then they will present an enormous document about 100 pages long and announce, "This is our latest market research report." Of course, it's a survey. It may be comprehensive to the nth degree, but it doesn't tell you much of value. Does it explain your customers' hierarchy of needs? Does it identify the key trends in your industry? Does it compare your profitability with your competitors'? While there's inherent value buried in a survey, just as there are hidden seams of gold in the raw ore, the insights only come out in the refining process of a Situation Analysis.

These nuggets of pure gold are what I call the "brutal truths." The brutal truths are those few crucial realities that you dare not ignore, because the consequences of doing so are brutal. These are the truths that will determine your destiny. Therein lies a vital, if counterintuitive, point: Finding the brutal truths is not only a pursuit of the new; it's a pursuit of the important. Describing the latest new thing is relatively easy. Sorting the important from the unimportant is much more demanding.

Winning the Battle for Insights

Winning the battle for insights is becoming tougher. As Paul Saffo, the noted futurist has observed, our predicament is the growing gap between the volume of information and our ability to make sense of it.[10]

As strategic leaders, we have to derive increasing simplicity from increasing complexity. Information is universally accessible and becoming free to all. The Internet offers it to us on a plate. No longer does the world belong to the ones with the most information, but to those with the highest ability to make sense of it; no longer to those who know more, but to those who understand better.

Consider the implications. For example, this tsunami of data presents daunting challenges to the intelligence agencies charged with keeping us safe. A recent public television program examined the work of the U.S. National Security Agency (NSA). The head of the NSA summarized this issue as follows: "We accumulate a massive stream of information, but it's hard to know what's there."[11] The national security game has changed from the production of information to drawing actionable insights from it. So, too, has the competitive challenge for all companies.

The maximum value of an insight occurs when you see it earlier and more clearly than your competitors do. The graphic in Figure 4.14 illustrates this point.

Let's take the 1962 Cuban missile crisis as an example. By the time the U.S. intelligence services realized what was happening, the Russian missiles armed with nuclear warheads were already installed in Cuba, 90 miles from the American coastline and pointed at U.S. targets. In *The Fog of War*, a documentary made some 40 years later, Robert McNamara, the Secretary of Defense at the time, describes in chilling detail what happens to your strategic options when you pick up the signals too late. Holding his thumb and forefinger a millimeter from each other, he revealed, "We came *this* close to destroying humanity. We just got lucky."

There is an inverse relationship between the strength of a signal and the range of options available to deal with it. The stronger the signal becomes, the weaker our ability to develop a favorable

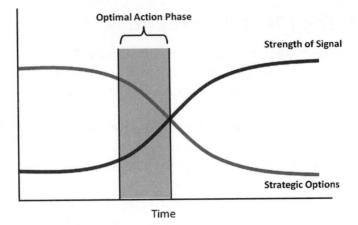

Figure 4.14 Winning the Battle for Insights

response. By the time the signal has become obvious to everyone, our options are lousy, as was so well illustrated by the missile crisis. (The crisis was eventually resolved by a behind-the-scenes deal between the United States and the Soviet Union, requiring the United States to make significant concessions to extricate itself.)

The same principles apply in business. Picking up the signals when they're obvious to everyone else gives you no advantage. You want to sharpen your antennae to capture weak signals, so that you have time to decide on the best course of action. GM was unable to interpret and respond to the early signals that consumers wanted highly energy-efficient cars. By the time it reacted, Toyota had taken a commanding position. GM was forced to play catch-up, and the strategic options available to the automaker were much worse than when the signal first appeared.

Albert Szent-Gyorgyi, the Nobel Prize-winning Hungarian biochemist, said, "Discovery consists of seeing what everyone has seen and thinking what nobody has thought."[12] Developing insights earlier and better than your competitors is one of the "killer competencies" identified in Chapter 3.

The Power of Synthesis

When summarizing the insights, the key is to find the story. A good Situation Analysis is never just a list of insights; it's a story that connects the pieces and makes the insights rich and real. When you put all the pieces together, you produce a synthesis. There's nothing so electrifying in the Situation Analysis process as when everyone in the team connects the dots.

Just as there is a big difference between information and insight, there's a gulf between analysis and synthesis. The word "analysis" comes from the Greek *analyein*, meaning to unravel. Analysis means breaking things down. Synthesis, on the other hand, means connecting things together—finding meaning in the relationship between things.

Research shows that strong analytical capabilities are very common among executives, whereas the ability to synthesize is rare.[13] This presents a problem. Most of the major advancements in the history of knowledge, such as Einstein's general theory of relativity, have been acts of synthesis rather than analysis. They involved seeing connections between things that had previously not been understood. Brian Greene, professor of physics and mathematics at Columbia University, called the general theory of relativity "the most beautiful scientific synthesis ever achieved."[14] Einstein himself believed that it is synthesis that reveals the really deep truths.

This is equally true in the battle for insights we face in business. Finding the brutal truths from a vast ocean of information most often involves synthesis, not just analysis. It's when we find the hidden relationships between things that we achieve deep insights and understand their implications more clearly.

Developing Our Synthesis Muscles

We don't have to be a genius like Einstein to create the "beauty of synthesis." We can use simple techniques to develop our "mental muscles" so we can outsynthesize our competitors.

I find it helpful to think of synthesis as having two dimensions: a vertical dimension that reveals historical trends and a horizontal dimension that reveals the connections between things.

The practical translation of this vertical/horizontal thinking is this: In doing a Situation Analysis, always be sure to map trends and avoid trying to develop an insight out of a snapshot. What was the reality yesterday? How did yesterday become today? How will today become tomorrow? The trends tell the story. That is the vertical dimension.

To reveal hidden connections and identify patterns, look horizontally. Examine the key insights from the separate areas of inquiry (customers, competitors, industry dynamics, etc.) and deliberately explore them to see how they are interconnected. You might say, for example, "Look how our market share has declined and hit our profits. We can see the cause of this in the lack of a compelling reason why customers should choose to do business with us. Our customers' needs have changed over time and our competitors have responded faster. They have outspent us on R&D and advertising and have better gross margins to fund these investments. This is a clear call to action for us to improve the benefits we offer our customers."

Doing a Great Situation Analysis: The Rules of Success

There are five key rules to bear in mind as you strive to excel at doing a Situation Analysis, listed in Figure 4.15:

---

❶ **Produce a diagnosis, not a survey.**
Dig beneath the symptoms to find the root causes. Filter the important from the unimportant. Show the key connections between things.

❷ **Trends tell a story; snapshots never do.**
When you make a significant finding, map the trend and tell the story it reveals.

❸ **Simplicity is a virtue.**
There is no such thing as a complicated insight. Sense-making must produce a crystal-clear answer. Simplicity is not a shortcut. It is very hard work.

❹ **Avoid jargon.**
Jargon is a substitute for thought. Produce insights that outsiders can understand. Use the language of the customer.

❺ **Consensus is the wrong objective.**
Aim for the best ideas to win, not to "average down."

Figure 4.15 Doing a Great Situation Analysis: The Rules of Success

Building the Bridge to the Strategic Choices

The point to remember is that Strategic Learning is an "insight to action" model. The sole objective of the Situation Analysis is to provide the insights that enable you to make the most intelligent choices on where you will compete and how you will win.

The insights from the Situation Analysis must lead you to the strategic choices in a coherent flow of logic. Just as the strategic choices represent the "what" of your strategy, the insights explain the "why." Strategic leaders must be able to construct that compelling logic if they are to mobilize the support of everyone in the organization. Here is a set of questions that will help you to build that bridge from your Situation Analysis to your strategic choices:

What are the brutal truths from the Situation Analysis?

The first task is to construct a clear and concise summary of the key insights, pulling together and synthesizing the work of the five Situation Analysis teams. The summary must be simple enough for the most junior person in your organization to understand. If you lose your people at this stage, they won't pay much attention to anything else.

What are the most important implications of these brutal truths?

This answers the "so what?" question. Why do these brutal truths matter to your organization? An insight is not complete until you can explain its implications. An effective way to define these implications is to answer these two questions:

▼ How are these brutal truths changing the rules of success in our industry?

▼ What threats and opportunities do they raise?

What are the key alternative courses of action we face?

Map out the main alternatives from which you will have to choose in making your strategic choices. Is there only one obvious way forward, or are there alternatives to be evaluated? Don't make a laundry list of every conceivable course of action. Confine your list to the credible alternatives that confront you.

What are the do-or-die challenges facing our organization?

Based on these questions, you should now be able to frame the key challenge or challenges that must be addressed in making your strategic choices. Effective leaders are those who are able to define the main challenges their organizations must deal with if they are to create a brilliant future.

A word of warning: It's easy to be confused by the flood of insights that emerge from a Situation Analysis. The key is to differentiate the important from the unimportant—to see clearly what matters most, as opposed to what is merely interesting. I offer the following advice from a surgeon whose skills I personally benefited from.

Three years ago, I had to undergo prostate surgery. Thankfully, all turned out well. I owe much to the skill and dedication of my surgeon, Dr. Ash Tewari, and his terrific team of residents. Ash's leadership skills are demonstrated by a simple guideline he repeats over and over to the aspiring young surgeons: "Always keep the main thing the main thing."

Smart leaders understand how to keep the main thing the main thing. They understand how to summarize and synthesize the insights from a Situation Analysis, focus on the most important ones, and leverage them into the next step in the Strategic Learning Cycle.

Focus

Clarifying Your Winning Proposition and Identifying Your Key Priorities

Our plans miscarry because they have no aim. When a man does not know what harbor he is making for, no wind is the right wind.

—Seneca

Winning the battle for insights is where competition begins. It is the basis for outsmarting your competitors. Lose this battle and you have lost the war. This is why generating superior insights is a killer competency.

The insights you generate must inform and inspire your choice-making, so you can move to the next step of the Strategic Learning Cycle: translating these insights into your Strategic Choices and Vision (Figure 5.1).

Making Your Strategic Choices

As you begin to move from insight to action, you'll need to use the results of your Situation Analysis to make your three Strategic

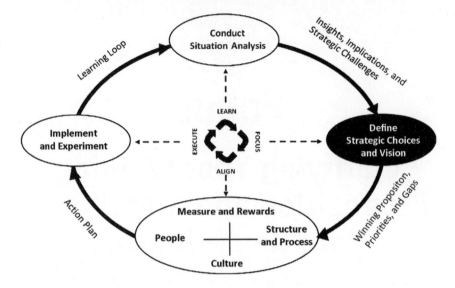

Figure 5.1 Leading through Strategic Learning: Focus

Choices: your Competitive Focus, your Winning Proposition, and your Key Priorities (Figure 5.2).

▼ Your *Competitive Focus* defines which markets and customers your firm will serve and which it will not. It specifies which products and/or services your firm will offer its chosen customers, and which it will not. These offerings are based on what is most important to your customers, as identified by the hierarchy of needs described in the Situation Analysis.

▼ The *Winning Proposition* is the heart of your firm's strategy. It defines what your firm will do differently or better than its competitors to achieve greater value for its customers and superior profits for itself—and hence greater value for its shareholders.

▼ The *Key Priorities* ensure that your firm's key resources will be concentrated behind your strategy. They define the most important things the firm will do to achieve the Winning Proposition—those few things that will make the biggest difference.

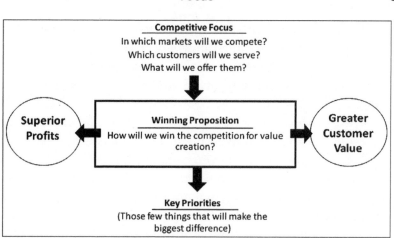

Figure 5.2 Translate Your Situation Analysis Insights into Your Strategic Choices

Strategic choice-making is in service of providing clarity on these three crucial issues, so that they provide a clear direction to your organization.

As you can see, the emphasis in all three elements is on focus. The challenge is to select a particular set of customers, a particular set of product or service offerings, a particular Winning Proposition, and a limited number of priorities. Every time you fail to choose, you're choosing to spend a percentage of your scarce resources on the wrong things. Your resources will be dissipated and wasted in a futile attempt to do everything at once, and you'll likely end up achieving nothing. Thus, one crucial litmus test of a good strategy is that the firm has decided not only what it *will* do but also what it will *not* do.

Of course, this process is a lot easier said than done. It takes courage to choose one course of action over another, and it takes fortitude to stick to your decision when the pressures of daily business tempt you to blur your focus. As Roger Enrico, ex-chairman of PepsiCo, put it, "The best decision is the right one. The second best decision is the wrong one. And the worst decision is *no* decision."[1]

The Parmenides Fallacy

Choice-making means wrestling with trade-offs. Yet we often fall into a decision trap by making a false comparison: We compare a possible future state with the present state. This is what Philip Bobbitt, a law professor at the University of Texas, calls the "Parmenides Fallacy," named after the Greek philosopher who mistakenly argued that the world was static and that all change was an illusion.[2]

The truth, of course, is that the world is dynamic, not static, and the present state is not a fixed point. So the basic rule of choice-making is that you should never compare a possible future state with the present state. The present state will be gone tomorrow. It will continue to evolve. When making a decision, always compare a future state with an alternative future state.

Here's a dramatic illustration of the Parmenides Fallacy in action. It's May 1945. Nazi Germany has surrendered and the focus now is on winning the war against Japan. The United States possesses a new and terrifyingly powerful weapon, an atomic bomb capable of incinerating entire cities and vaporizing their populations. The estimated casualties from dropping the bomb on the initial target of Hiroshima: 150,000 civilians killed and hundreds of thousands maimed. Can a government condone such a horrifying act and still hope to retain any moral integrity?

Some of those arguing against dropping the bomb fell victim to the Parmenides Fallacy: They assumed that not dropping the bomb would create zero casualties. They estimated the cost of acting but they didn't calculate the cost of not acting. In the emotional debates that followed, President Harry Truman kept his cool and asked the intelligent question: "What would be the alternative to dropping the bomb and what would the casualty count be?"

The alternative future state was even more horrifying. Withholding the bomb meant a ground invasion of the Japanese home islands by American forces. After bloody battles up the Pacific island chain, culminating in a huge butcher's bill at Iwo Jima and Okinawa, there was no doubt that an invasion would be horrendously costly: Estimated casualties were calculated at more than half a million American soldiers on the main island of Kyushu alone *and* untold numbers of Japanese. The real comparison was not 150,000 versus a present state of zero; it was 150,000 versus the alternative future state of millions of American and Japanese lives.

Truman's dilemma has since been examined by hundreds of scholars and by countless debating societies. It's worth bringing up again in the context of the Strategic Learning model because it illustrates the often-agonizing conundrums at the heart of strategic choice-making.

The Parmenides Fallacy frequently sneaks into businesses' strategic decisions, especially when companies are considering the introduction of a new product. Those arguing for it will point out the great potential of this innovation if it were to succeed. All too often, though, an opposing voice will make a beguiling counterargument, "But that would cannibalize our existing business, and at lower margins to boot." That argument could stop the innovation in its tracks, and leave a company forever clinging to its base business, while competitors innovate successfully.

The right question to ask in weighing such a decision is, "What will happen if we *do not* introduce this new product?" This opens up an examination of this alternative future state. If a new product is an attractive opportunity, competitors are very likely to launch it sooner or later. So the real comparison is "Should we cannibalize our own business or allow competitors to do it to us?" The smart choice then becomes a matter of managing cannibalization rather than trying vainly to avoid it.

That was the challenge that Intel took on in the mid-1980s. Until then, Intel was the company to beat in the memory chip market segment. As company cofounder and former CEO Andy Grove wrote in *Only the Paranoid Survive*, "Intel . . . stood for memories; conversely, memories meant . . . Intel." Then, Japanese memory producers appeared, with higher-quality, lower-priced, mass-produced chips. At the same time, a business slump hit the memory chip market. Intel began hemorrhaging money. The Japanese moved in for the kill.

As Grove described the situation, Intel had two key options. They could continue to compete against the Japanese in the memory chip market, even though it was obviously a losing battle. Or they could get out of the memory chip market entirely and place all their bets on an emerging technology invented at the company 10 years earlier: microprocessors.

Microprocessors had great potential. Intel's microprocessor was designed into the original IBM PC and became the standard for subsequent PC designs, both for IBM and IBM's competitors. At the time, though, personal computers were just a few steps past novelty items, and microprocessors represented a slower-growing, smaller-volume market than memory chips. Only in hindsight can we see the inevitable and overwhelming acceptance of personal computers.

Nonetheless, having concluded that they were confronting a future state of probable extinction if they continued on their previous course, Intel boldly committed to microprocessors. By the early 1990s, owing mostly to their success with microprocessors and a surging worldwide demand for PCs, Intel had become the largest semiconductor company in the world, larger than even the Japanese companies that had beaten them in memories. "Had we dithered longer, we could have missed our chance at all this," Grove wrote. "We might have vacillated between a heroic effort to hang on to our dwindling share of the memory business and an effort that might have been too weak to project us into the exploding microprocessor market. Had we stayed indecisive, we might have lost both."

The reality is that there is no such thing as a nondecision. Inaction is itself a decision that carries its own consequences. It must, therefore, be a deliberate decision rather than something that happens by default. As decision makers, we constantly underestimate the risks of doing nothing.

Let's refer back to the questions posed in translating Situation Analysis insights into strategic choices. Intel's example demonstrates just how difficult answering those questions can be. If Intel abandoned the memory market, which markets *would* it compete in? Which customers *would* it serve? What *would* it offer them? And how could it win the competition for value creation?

Today, of course, Intel is known as *the* microprocessor company. "Intel Inside" is one of the most recognized logos in brand marketing, right up there with Coca-Cola and Nike. But the process of getting there was scary and fraught with doubts and trade-offs.

In choosing among alternative future states, there are no guarantees of success. The only pathway to success depends on having clarity about the risks and opportunities about each of the options, thereby enabling you to choose the best Winning Proposition and the Key Priorities for success.

Value Proposition versus Winning Proposition

The centerpiece of your strategy is your organization's Winning Proposition. Figure 5.3 reiterates the definition.

All successful implementation journeys start with this level of luminous clarity as the springboard for action. Everything that follows is energized by a clear line of sight back to the Winning Proposition, which represents the core of your strategy. Always keep the main thing the main thing. Unless you have this clarity of focus in place, don't even think about implementation. All you will have is confusion.

In Chapter 2, I emphasized the difference between a Value Proposition and a Winning Proposition. This is not simply a matter of semantics. It is a difference of ideas.

The governing reality here is that all value is relative. In a competitive world where customers have choices, absolute definitions of value have no meaning. Competitive advantage comes from creating *greater* value for our customers than the competing alternatives, and then converting that into superior profits. We have to "mind the gap."

The Centerpiece of Strategy

An organization's **Winning Proposition** defines how it will win the competition for value creation, by answering these questions:

❶ What unique benefits will we deliver to our customers that provide a compelling reason for them to do business with us?

❷ How will we translate this exceptional customer value into superior financial returns for our enterprise?

Figure 5.3 Winning Proposition: Definition

A Value Proposition may be easier to define but it aims only at participating. A Winning Proposition aims at finding, defining, and exploiting the decisive margin of difference. Discovering that crucial margin of difference, measuring its impact, and then constantly stretching the gap lies at the heart of superior performance. In Darwinian terms, the Winning Proposition is the favorable variation that spells the difference between survival and extinction.

When we think about the concept of winning, we sometimes resort to sporting analogies. In some ways this can be useful, for example in understanding the role of teamwork. But in an important way, this can be dangerous. Let's take basketball. The teams strive to score points against each other. The winning team is the one with the most points at the end. The whole idea here is to score points *against your competitor*. But business is different. You don't win by scoring points *against* your competitor. You win by scoring more points *for your customer* than your competitor does. This involves a kind of triangulation: Do more for your customers than your competitors do, then no matter what threats they pose, you will beat them.

Food distribution giant Sysco scores points for its customers not just by selling supplies but by helping its customers run their restaurants profitably.[3] On-time delivery of items like clean napkins and ketchup are the table stakes. Once that need is satisfied, every restaurant wants to move up the hierarchy of needs: They want to provide a memorable experience—delicious food served by pleasant waiters in an enticing ambience—and make money doing it. In these tough economic times, Sysco offers a way for restaurant owners to thrive in the business they love.

In addition to selling a vast array of supplies, Sysco includes in its service offering to its customers a free consulting service called the Business Review. The company has turned its test kitchens into cooking schools where Sysco chefs show client restaurants how to create more delicious food offerings while slashing their budgets. Other elements in the program include redesigning menus to showcase the most profitable items and coaching waitstaff to encourage patrons to visit more often and order more when they do. With 15,000 restaurants estimated to shut down during the recession,

Sysco is betting that the Business Review will keep its customers alive and lead to greater market share for itself.

The answer, then, to question 1 of the Winning Proposition— What unique benefits will we deliver to our customers that will provide a compelling reason for them to do business with us?—comes down to triangulation. You don't win by taking aim at a competitor. You win by scoring more points for your customer than that competitor does. In short, you beat your competitor by going to your customer. In offering a package of integrated solutions, rather than packages of supplies, Sysco demonstrates how well it understands its customers' needs. It's as simple as that.

An actionable Winning Proposition must harness the force of simplicity. In the words of poet Robert Southey, "It is with words as with sunbeams. The more they are condensed, the deeper they burn."[4] Don't strangle the essence in a welter of words and qualifying clauses. That's what newspaper editors call "burying the lead." Avoid the use of technical words and jargon. Use straightforward everyday language that everyone in your organization will easily understand. The discipline is to simplify and crystallize and keep working it over until you capture your strategic focus in as few words as possible.

It's worth repeating some of the examples mentioned earlier:

In Columbia Business School's executive education programs, our strategy flows from a simple truth: an idea, no matter how brilliant, has no value until it has been put into action. Therefore our commitment to our customers is, *"We will bring you the best ideas relevant to your needs coupled with powerful tools to convert these ideas into action."* Everything we do ensures that we deliver on that promise.

Starbucks aims at providing a superior customer experience. It captures this central idea in this compelling mantra: *"We are not in the coffee business serving people. We are in the people business serving coffee."*[5] What a great way to remind all Starbucks employees in plain words what to focus on day in and day out.

Where Does Your Vision Fit In?

A vision is essentially a statement of what you aim to become. "Shouldn't everything start with a statement of our vision?" I'm often asked. I really don't think that's a good idea.

Trying to invent a vision *before* doing the Situation Analysis is like shooting in the dark. It ensures that the vision is based on whim, rather than on insight. After all, the insights from the Situation Analysis are designed to inform everything else that follows. There is nothing more frustrating or counterproductive than conducting a visioning exercise in a vacuum, with absolutely no shared context.

Working on a vision statement as part of the next step *after* the Situation Analysis is fair game. However, my experience has been that the best time to define a vision is after you have spelled out your Winning Proposition. At that point, you can ask yourself the question, "If we deliver our Winning Proposition brilliantly well, where can it take us in the future?" That aspirational statement will represent your vision. It will also have the virtue of being logically connected to your Winning Proposition, providing a much more coherent and compelling leadership statement. The alternative of doing it as an independent exercise seldom works as well.

Of course, many companies already have a vision statement in place when they tackle their strategy. Where a clear and compelling vision already exists, going through the Strategic Learning process is a good opportunity either to validate what you already have or update it in the light of changing circumstances.

Delivering Superior Profits

You are well on the road to creating a Winning Proposition if you can answer question 1: *What unique benefits will we deliver to our customers that provide a compelling reason for them to do business with us?*

But that's not enough. A Winning Proposition embraces two key ideas: superior customer value and superior economic value. So you must be able to convincingly answer question 2: *How will we translate this exceptional customer value into superior financial returns for our enterprise?*

It is futile to generate superior value for customers if you don't convert this value into superior profits. Naturally, your customers have little concern for how much profit you make, as long as you are there for them in the long term. They only want to hear your answer to question 1. But your shareholders certainly want to know your answer to question 2, and you won't have a sustainable business unless you can achieve financial excellence. The challenge is the ability to deliver on both counts.

Creating superior value for customers and generating superior profits are profoundly interconnected. Greater customer value invariably expresses itself through advantages in price and volume. The greater the value you deliver to customers, the more your volume and relative price will grow. That gives you a competitive numerator. But you also have to work on your denominator: costs and assets. The wider you can stretch the elastic band between the value you provide to your customers and the costs you incur in doing so, the greater your competitive advantage and the higher your profits.

How do you know whether you are achieving superior profits? The truth is that many companies complicate this issue to the point that operating managers—the people who actually have to deliver the profits—get stuck in a quagmire of overmeasurement and financial technicalities. The result is, they lose the understanding of what is actually driving their firm's or their division's economic engine. And if they don't understand this, they won't be able to make smart strategic choices.

The basic arithmetic of a business is actually very simple. In operational terms, there are only three moving parts in any business: revenue, costs, and assets. Arithmetically, think of revenue as the numerator, and costs and assets as the denominator. Picturing this as an equation, the idea is to make the number on the right side of the equal sign as big as possible. In Chapter 2, I described the value/cost gap; this simple equation is a financial depiction of it (see Figure 5.4).

Financial performance is everyone's business for a very basic reason: Everything you do in a business should either raise value or reduce costs or help other parts of the organization do the same. No

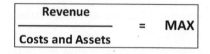

Figure 5.4   A Crucial Formula: The Arithmetic of Business

matter what your position is in an organization, you should understand the impact you have on profitability. People in a procurement or manufacturing department can have a direct effect on lowering costs and assets; similarly, people in sales have a direct impact on raising revenue. But supporting functions, such as HR or IT or the controller's office, aren't exempt, even though their contribution may be indirect. Their ultimate purpose is to enable the organization through their efforts to make the number on the right-hand side of the equation as big as possible. In short, whatever you do should be aimed at either raising the revenue numerator or lowering the costs and assets denominator.

For a manager, making decisions based on this clear financial line of sight is no different from making choices based on a clear strategic line of sight. The financial line of sight is a companion to the strategic line of sight; both should flow naturally from the organization's strategic goals and converge into a powerful single strategy. Each of these converging lines of sight should be simple and straightforward enough so that if you pose the question, "Why am I (or you) doing this?" you should produce an uncomplicated answer that supports the basic equation.

I can't stress enough that winning means creating both superior customer *and* economic value, and that the same emphasis must be placed on each element in your Winning Proposition. Just thinking about how to boost the organization's financials is incomplete; and just thinking about how you will drive superior value for your customers is incomplete. Your organization has a Winning Proposition *only* if it is able to integrate the two elements and satisfy both.

People often say, "In this company, it's all a numbers game." By that, they mean the company develops its plans by focusing *solely* on the numbers, rather than on customers and ideas, and *then* incorporating the numbers. The danger with this approach is that once you get into that mold, the people who are good at numbers get promoted to the top; when the ground shifts and customers have a richer source of choices, it's tough for a leadership team with inbuilt biases that are all about numbers to make the switch. They're used to speaking a language of superior profits, not a language of superior value.

You can't serve the shareholder at the expense of the customer, nor can you serve the customer at the expense of the shareholder. You have to create synergy between the two.

How do you know whether you're generating superior financial results? That's where the three bottom lines come in.

All the operating profit ratios that matter can be derived from that one simple equation shown in Figure 5.4:

▼ Revenue minus Costs = Profit

▼ Profit divided by Revenue = Return on Sales (ROS)

▼ Profit divided by Assets = Return on Assets (ROA)

There is only one key number you cannot derive from this equation: cash flow. The reason is a mismatch of timing. You often have to spend money on costs and assets before the associated revenue comes in. Therefore, in order to understand your financial performance, you must also measure operating cash flow.

The Three Bottom Lines

By looking at these basic measures, operating managers are able to assess the financial performance of their businesses by answering these three fundamental questions:

▼ Are we generating satisfactory profits? Look at your ROS.

▼ Are we achieving a satisfactory return on the assets employed? Look at your ROA.

▼ Are we converting our profits into cash? Look at your operating cash flow.

What emerges from this is that there is not just one bottom line. There are *three* bottom lines: ROS, ROA, and cash flow. You cannot improve the financial performance of your business unless you understand and achieve excellence on all three bottom lines.

A Winning Proposition requires that you achieve *superior* financial returns from the choices you have made. This is a comparative measure. How can you determine whether or not you are doing this? I suggest there are three benchmarks of excellence that will tell you unarguably whether your profitability is truly superior. They are:

▼ *Your three bottom lines are better than your competitors'.* This means that you are constantly measuring and comparing the profit performance of your key competitors and know where you stand in relation to them. Companies that don't do this are flying in the dark. As described in Chapter 4, a good financial analyst will be able to do this with impressive accuracy, and then get better and better over time. Remember that a more profitable competitor will have the resources to outspend and outcompete you.

▼ *Your ROA is greater than your cost of capital.* The cost of capital for your business is essentially the blended average cost of debt plus equity—what amounts to the expectations of investors based on their opportunity costs. Don't forget, investors have choices. A practical way to think about the cost of capital is that it is the cost of using other people's money. The cost of capital is a fundamental benchmark of performance, and any company's treasurer should be able to compute this number. Returns greater than your cost of capital create value. Those lower than your cost of capital destroy value. This is an inescapable reality. Consistently outperforming your cost of capital will attract investors and lower your costs of raising money in the capital markets.

▼ *Your performance trends are positive.* A key benchmark is your own past performance. A snapshot tells you nothing. Trends tell the story. I'm surprised at how many companies simply look at this year's performance versus budget or versus the prior year. The only real way to know how well you are doing is to look at the five-year trend; that way, you can interpret your trajectory and make the right midcourse corrections.

To summarize, a simple way to remember the financial basics is to think three by three: three bottom lines measured against three benchmarks. The evidence shows convincingly that if you exceed these benchmarks on these key measures, your shareholders will prosper.

Explanatory note: For profits, I am using earnings before interest and tax, usually referred to as EBIT. For assets, I am using physical assets, the fixed and net current assets on the balance sheet—that is, property, plant, and equipment, plus inventory and receivables, minus payables. These are the elements for which operating executives should be held accountable. At an enterprise level, there will of course be overall measures such as return on invested capital (ROIC) and return on equity (ROE), the latter being much more a matter of financial engineering.

Your Key Priorities

There is no more important statement in your strategy than your Winning Proposition. It must state clearly and simply how you will win the competition for value creation: both customer value and economic value. You cannot lead your organization without it.

But to create an intense focus on the right things and gear your organization up for action, your Winning Proposition alone is not enough. You must also define the things that will get you there. How will you concentrate and mobilize your scarce resources to realize your Winning Proposition? You now need to define your Key Priorities, those vital few things the entire organization must focus on, day in and day out, with passion and relentless determination to achieve success.

The 80/20 Rule

Few concepts are as widely misunderstood as priorities.

Most executives are familiar with what has come to be called the 80/20 rule but few can articulate what it really means or live by its dictates. The 80/20 principle was famously articulated by an Italian economist called Vilfredo Pareto (1848–1923). Pareto discovered in his studies of the British economy a surprising imbalance. About 80 percent of the wealth was created by 20 percent of the population.[6] This shocked him, and at first he thought this was an aberration of British culture. But his subsequent studies showed that it was a more general principle of economics, not just a peculiarity of the British.

This principle of "unequal distribution" has since been found to be a universal truth, not just confined to economics. Joseph Juran, the quality guru, described it as "the rule of the vital few." This same idea was applied just as strongly by the other major leader of the quality revolution, W. Edwards Deming. The history and evolution of this important concept is described with great clarity by Richard Koch in his book *The 80/20 Principle*. Here are the basic principles of the 80/20 rule:

▼ There is always an imbalance between inputs and outputs.

▼ The majority of inputs will have very little effect on the desired result.

▼ A small minority (the Vital Few) will make a hugely disproportionate difference to the result.

▼ Identifying and leveraging the Vital Few is essential to the success of any endeavor.

Figure 5.5 offers some examples of the 80/20 rule mentioned by Richard Koch in his book.

How can you harness the awesome power of the 80/20 rule to drive success in your organization? Think of your Key Priorities as "those vital few things that will make the biggest difference to the achievement of our Winning Proposition."

- 20% of software code drives
  80% of the usage
- 15% of world population uses
  80% of the energy
- 25% of world population owns
  80% of the wealth
- 28% of beer drinkers drink
  80% of the beer
- 5% of U.S. households own
  75% of the equity
- 1.3% of movies earned
  80% of the box office*

  * Study of 300 new releases over 18 months

Figure 5.5   Examples of the 80/20 Rule

How many priorities should there be? My rule of thumb is *between 3 and 5, but never more than 5.* I often see lists of 8 or 10 things called "priorities." This is a contradiction in terms. A list that long is a laundry list. People cannot even remember what they are, let alone act on them. It produces the exactly opposite effect of what a strategy must do for you. Employees become swamped by complexity. Confusion reigns. It's as if the leader is saying "I haven't a clue what's important. I'm lost in the jungle." Remember the simple dictum of chef Marco Pierre White in Chapter 3: Complexity creates confusion, confusion creates inconsistency, and inconsistency creates failure.

There is no more crucial work in strategy than defining the Key Priorities. The unforgiving reality is that the longer your list of priorities, the less chance you have of achieving any of them.

The Gearbox Parable

The 80/20 rule teaches us that the most important task of leadership is to provide the right priorities for your organization to pursue. To illustrate that, I'd like to use an example provided by the CEO of one of the largest enterprises in the world, shown in Figure 5.6.

I was running a seminar for a group of senior executives from this company when, in a Q&A session, the CEO got into the issue of

Figure 5.6 The Parable of the Gearbox

effective leadership. "What does it feel like to be the head of one of the largest companies in the world?" he was asked. "Well, I'll tell you," he replied. "I feel as though I have my hands on a large wheel with cogs connecting to smaller and smaller wheels below. It's like a gearbox. Every time I turn the large wheel, even just one notch, all the smaller wheels turn faster and faster. The smaller wheels represent all of you. My job is to make sure that I turn the big wheel on exactly the right issues, so all the smaller wheels are spinning on the few things that matter most. Wherever you are in this organization, you also have your hands on a wheel and that wheel is engaged with a series of smaller wheels. Your job as leaders is to turn your wheel on those same issues so you set those smaller wheels spinning on the vital few priorities for success."

The 80/20 rule says that a very few things have a disproportionate impact on outcome. The gearbox parable is all about defining the few things that matter most and galvanizing your organization to act on those priorities. As you mobilize the 80/20 rule, you need to be very strategic about what you ask your organization to do so that when you turn the big wheel all the smaller wheels will spin on the right things.

That's why you should limit your Key Priorities to three to five items, and *no more* than five items. It's very easy to authorize an initiative every time you think of something that would be nice to do; it's so easy that it even has its own term: *mission creep*. Every time you give in to mission creep, you dilute something else. As a leader, you're creating overload and confusion. You're not keeping the main thing the main thing. And no matter what your role, if you are not maintaining a clear line of sight to the organization's Winning Proposition and focusing the energies of your people to support it, then the Winning Proposition is reduced to empty words, and no strategy will work.

How the Girl Scouts Did It

The following example illustrates the process—often difficult but ultimately rewarding—of how to use the Situation Analysis to define a Winning Proposition and Key Priorities.

In 2004, when I first began working with the Girl Scouts of the USA (GSUSA) as a strategic advisor, the organization was facing a gradual but consistent decline in membership, particularly among its teenage members. Girls' lives had changed radically since Girl Scouts was founded almost 100 years ago. The Internet, cell phones, shopping malls, soccer, and many other alternatives were competing for girls' time and commitment.

The Girl Scouts' CEO, Kathy Cloninger, had visited Canada and Australia and gotten a shock. In both countries, a slow decline in membership, similar to the gradual trend then occuring in the United States, had suddenly shifted into a headlong downward plunge. In both countries, Girl Scouts (referred to there as Girl Guides) had all but disappeared. There had occurred what Malcolm Gladwell would refer to as a tipping point from gradual to sudden, from chronic to acute, after which point recovery becomes all but impossible. Kathy realized that the time had come for decisive action. Girl Scouts was in need of a transformation.

Their Situation Analysis identified these brutal truths: "We confront a crisis of relevance. We are being pushed by the past rather than pulled by the future. We have no clear unifying theme or rallying point. If we don't address these issues, we risk going on autopilot to long-term decline."

A dedicated, cross-functional, core strategy group of 26 Girl Scouts executives gathered to crystallize the insights from the Situation Analysis. First, they had to define who their customers were: Were they girls? Parents? Volunteers? All of them?

The answer eventually coalesced: "Girl Scouts exists to serve girls. Those are our customers. Everything we do must serve the needs of girls."

This led to an existential question: "If we exist to serve girls, then what, at its essence, do we seek to do for them?" The programmatic activities were obvious: camps, troop activities, life skills, cookie sales. But surely these things were a means to an end, not ends in themselves? What we were actually reexamining was the mission of Girl Scouts, that wellspring from which all else flows.

What emerged was a bright beacon that would light the way forward. The core of the Girl Scouts mission is to develop girls as leaders, and its overarching goal is to be the *premier* leadership experience for girls.

This was not so much brand-new as it was clarifying and reaffirming. Rallying behind this leadership development mission would unify Girl Scouts as a movement. All their energies and efforts would be concentrated on bringing this mission to life.

In translating this mission into action, the Girl Scouts understood a crucial reality. Girls are their customers, and customers have choices. The organization summed up this central challenge as follows: "We must give girls what they *need* in ways that they *want*." In other words, they needed to define their Winning Proposition.

Figure 5.7 shows the Winning Proposition created by the Girl Scouts.

Girl Scouting builds girls of courage, confidence, and character who make the world a better place.

Figure 5.7 Girl Scouts' Winning Proposition

The next task was to do the crucial diagnostic work: identify the critical drivers of success and define how to concentrate the scarce resources of the organization on the few things that would make the biggest difference to the outcome. This filled the leadership with a deep sense of responsibility. How would they turn the big wheel on just the right issues so the smaller wheels would spin faster and faster on what mattered most? The realization set in that this was going to be a pivotal moment.

The Girl Scouts is a large, diverse organization, with (at that time) more than 300 local councils spread throughout the country, each with a largely independent legal status, but bound together as a movement pursuing their shared mission. It is broadly similar to a franchise operation such as McDonald's, but of course it operates in the nonprofit sector. The organization is served by almost 1 million volunteers, who are highly committed but who feel a strong sense of individual ownership over what should be done. If the core strategy team could not get the priorities right and then achieve buy-in from the whole organization, little of consequence would happen. If the Girl Scouts fell short of creating an intense focus on the vital few, it would have scant hope of pulling off the major transformation that was the key to its long-term survival.

Clearly, identifying the Key Priorities would not be a five-minute exercise of making a list on a flipchart. There was an intense debate marked by challenge and counterchallenge. We found ourselves going back to the Situation Analysis to remind ourselves of the brutal truths that we dared not ignore, such as the fact that Girl Scouts suffers from a crisis of relevance, and that the brand image would have to be rebuilt. Without the hard work that had gone into the Situation Analysis, it would have been impossible to do this crucial diagnostic work.

Girl Scouts has a history of operating by consensus, and often they were tempted to add items to the list to placate some loud voices pleading for their favorite initiative. To her great credit, CEO Kathy Cloninger stuck to her guns. The Girl Scouts would base its transformation on no more than five key priorities, which would define the difference between success and failure. These priorities

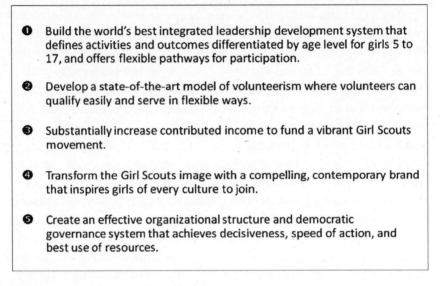

❶ Build the world's best integrated leadership development system that defines activities and outcomes differentiated by age level for girls 5 to 17, and offers flexible pathways for participation.

❷ Develop a state-of-the-art model of volunteerism where volunteers can qualify easily and serve in flexible ways.

❸ Substantially increase contributed income to fund a vibrant Girl Scouts movement.

❹ Transform the Girl Scouts image with a compelling, contemporary brand that inspires girls of every culture to join.

❺ Create an effective organizational structure and democratic governance system that achieves decisiveness, speed of action, and best use of resources.

Figure 5.8 Girl Scouts' Strategic Priorities

would be couched in language that everyone could understand. Each priority would powerfully support the Winning Proposition, and working in combination they would be a clarion call for focused action.

The acid test was to step back and ask the decisive question: "If we do these five things brilliantly well, will we achieve our Winning Proposition?" When the answer was a convincing yes, the next step was to lay out these priorities with simple clarity on one page. They are listed in Figure 5.8.

Girl Scouts now operates with a collective understanding that everything they do will be in furtherance of their mission, Winning Proposition, and Key Priorities. Remarkable work has been done. In just five years, they have created a state-of-the-art leadership development experience for girls at every age level, one that promises to make a profound difference to the leadership capacity of women in the United States. Fulfilling their mission is universally inspiring because, after all, there is no higher calling than bringing out the full potential of others.

Deciding What Not to Do

The toughest part of creating clarity of focus is deciding what not to do. Organizations are great at piling things on, but not at subtracting things. There is always someone not wanting to let go. The result is a swamping effect, which either slows down everything else or paralyzes the organization. Nobody understands what is important and what isn't. There is no clear sense of direction. The organization then begins to run in place more and more rapidly, as opposed to moving forward. Bureaucracy sets in. Now it's work for the sake of work.

To avoid this outcome, we must have an analytical framework for deciding what to eliminate or downplay, and what to emphasize. Otherwise, this process becomes a subjective tug-of-war. In the Situation Analysis, as part of Own Realities, I always recommend the simple framework of the Portfolio Profitability Map illustrated in Chapter 4. This provides the necessary rigor for deciding what not to do.

The Geranium Story

I'm reminded of this lesson every spring when my wife and I plant the window boxes on the balconies in front of our respective offices in our New York apartment. We both like to plant geraniums, and without becoming too competitive, I couldn't help but notice that her geraniums were much healthier; the leaves were much lusher and the plants produced more flowers than mine. We had started with the exact same flowers on the exact same day, and the window boxes receive the exact same amount of sun, so why were hers such a blooming picture of health and mine looking so scrawny? Was she watering them differently? Fertilizing them? Talking to them?

As it turned out, she did have a secret weapon, which she generously told me when I couldn't stand it any longer and asked. It was her scissors. She grabbed them and a garbage bag, and ferociously began hacking away at my weakling plants. "Stop, please!" I shouted. "You're destroying my garden." "No, I'm creating it," she countered. "Just wait a week and you'll see."

I counted off the days and I couldn't believe what emerged from the carnage. It was the most beautiful set of geraniums I had ever had. Now they're a source of immense pride. They're also a reminder of the lesson about focus. My wife's willingness to ruthlessly wield her scissors to deadhead spent flowers and prune unproductive stems enabled the plant to concentrate its life forces on producing new flowers from the healthiest stems.

The geranium analogy applies to every living system, whether it's a garden or a business. Whenever you remove the underperforming parts of any system, all the life forces of that system become concentrated on the few things that matter most, and that system will flourish.

Deadheading isn't a one-time activity. You're always clearing away the unnecessary undergrowth. Peter Drucker recommended that at least every three years every product or initiative in your organization should be put on trial for its life.

A major issue for a pharmaceutical business I work with is the effectiveness of its R&D efforts. In fact, if you want to place a value on a pharmaceutical company, you start by examining the value of its research pipeline. If it doesn't have a rich pipeline, the business is going to hit a wall. But it doesn't make sense for an R&D division to pursue every idea. As any plumber will happily tell you, if you keep adding initiatives to the pipeline and not taking things out, the pipeline will clog and the promising initiatives will get held up along with the not-so-promising ones. The more time chewed up in the pipeline, the less time you have to commercialize your innovation. This makes it absolutely vital for the R&D executives to regularly examine the products and decide which to keep and which to kill.

It's very tough for R&D scientists to give up a project. They're driven by the promise of success and are always hoping that tomorrow will bring a breakthrough. That's the nature of being dedicated. You need courage *and* a rigorous methodology that regularly puts each project or product on trial for its life.

I asked the managers of this company whether they measured their kill rate. They kind of smiled and said, "Not explicitly." They knew how many candidates they had added to the pipeline but they didn't know how many they had killed. That's a surefire way of drowning high-potential candidates in the clutter. "You know what the problem is?" they said. "A few years ago, we decided to discontinue one of the research projects on a particular drug. We sold off the rights to that drug to another company. And that company turned it into a blockbuster. So people are very gun-shy now."

Mark Twain said that a cat that sits on a hot stove will never sit on a hot stove again. But it won't sit on a cold stove, either. Similarly, this pharmaceutical company was scared to tinker with its pipeline; for fear of losing out on a blockbuster, it made the mistake of holding on to *all* its candidates. It had allowed itself to be trapped by the Parmenides Fallacy. When making a decision, always compare a future state with an alternative future state, never with the present state.

The question every company has to address is, "How can we get smarter about pruning when one mistake can make us gun-shy?"

The reality is you're always going to make mistakes. There is no such thing as a guarantee or certainty in business or life; you're backing probabilities. In making strategic choices, the right bet is *not* on trying to eliminate mistakes but on maximizing your focus.

How do you increase the probability that you are focused on the right issues? The responsibility for identifying which activities to kill and which to encourage should pervade the entire organization. If you are below the level of the CEO, what guides your hand is a clear line of sight back to the organization's Key Priorities.

In making these decisions about focus, you have to answer two questions:

▼ What are we going to do?

▼ What are we not going to do?

If you don't answer the second question, you won't have clear focus, because you can't constantly add things without subtracting. You will always be better off in the long run if you err on the side of focus and eliminate as much as you can. You're betting on probabilities; while you may miss one or two opportunities, if you are focusing on the right things in the aggregate, you are more likely to make the right bets. Painful as it is for me to get out my pruning scissors,

I now know that if I cut my geraniums consistently and intelligently, I'll have a better garden.

Subtract, Then Multiply

The two most powerful forces in the world are: focus and compounding (Figure 5.9). These two forces release their power only when you multiply the one by the other. Working on their own they have very little impact. But the combination is unbeatable.

How do you harness them to work for your organization?

Focus is what you get when you have defined your Winning Proposition and Key Priorities and are utterly clear about what you are not going to do. That clarity of focus is your springboard.

What about compounding? Let me explain what I mean by this. Let's start by examining the effect of financial compounding, the simple process of reinvesting the income on an investment and watching your principal grow. Over time, it grows exponentially. For example, if you take $100 per month ($3 per day) from age 25 to age 65 and stash it under your mattress, you will end up with $48,000. But if you invest the same amount at 8 percent annual interest rate and reinvest the interest, you will end up with $300,000. The $300,000 is six times greater, because of the compounding effect you get when you reinvest the income—which is why Einstein was said

FOCUS x COMPOUNDING

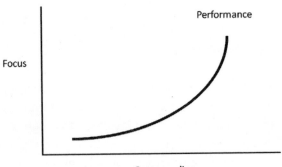

Figure 5.9 The Two Most Powerful Forces in the World

to have called compound interest the most powerful force in the universe.

But I am not talking of financial compounding here. I am talking about reinvesting the *learning*. The exponential effect is exactly the same, however. You create this effect only if you start with a crystal-clear focus on your Winning Proposition and Key Priorities. Then, through a process of deliberate practice you constantly improve on these few things, thereby reinvesting the learning.

This reinvestment of learning is like a surfer catching a wave. It picks up extra force and generates the difference between doing and excelling. When you do this, you make it extremely hard for any competitor to catch up with you. This is what ExxonMobil has done on safety and project excellence, what Tiger Woods has done in golf and, what Marco Pierre White did in cooking.

The story of success is always the same. In these two essentials it never varies. The vital difference between winners and losers can be boiled down to a simple equation: Subtract all extraneous distractions then multiply the result through learning. Subtract, *then* multiply. Focus × Compounding = Excellence.

Align

Mobilizing Your Entire Organization behind Your Strategy

Sticks in a bundle are unbreakable.

—African proverb

W hen I was growing up in South Africa, the rural African children helped to collect firewood every evening. It was a ritual that had existed for millennia and shaped tribal culture, as encapsulated in the above proverb. I can just imagine an elder teaching its lesson to the next generation. "Do you see this stick? Take it. Break it. Was that easy? Yes. Now take five sticks. Take them. Break them." And after the youngster gave up in frustration, the elder would say, "Exactly. Sticks in a bundle are unbreakable."

To African elders, the proverb illustrates that the power of a tribe is much greater than that of one individual member. To businesspeople, it represents the power of every person and all the elements of the business system working together in support of a

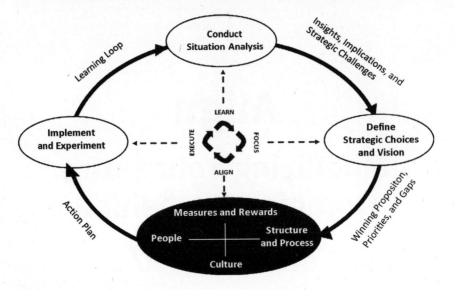

Figure 6.1 Leading through Strategic Learning: Align

shared purpose: the immense potential generated by aligned action in implementing a strategy. Leaders accomplish nothing on their own. It's when they mobilize collective action that things happen.

We're now at the stage in the Strategic Learning cycle (Figure 6.1) where we are making the transition from strategy creation to strategy implementation. You have generated superior insights through your Situation Analysis, and translated those into a crystal-clear Winning Proposition and Key Priorities. Having moved successfully from *Learn* to *Focus*, your challenge now is to effectively *Align* and *Execute*. Identifying and overcoming the pitfalls in your path are crucial to closing the larger gap between doing and excelling.

Leading a Journey

Wouldn't it be nice if you could simply ask your organization for effective implementation the same way you would order room service in a hotel? Dial 9 and request your desired result. "Our pleasure," the voice would say. "Delivery will be in half an hour."

As we know, this "dial it in" approach to leadership hardly ever works. Once you've defined your strategy, it's very tempting to hold a pep rally, or its corporate equivalent, which is to call a major meeting and do a brilliant presentation. Having gotten your people all excited about your Winning Proposition and Key Priorities, you dust off your hands and say, "Now go off and do it." Unfortunately, a one-shot speech, no matter how passionate, at a one-shot conference is the equivalent of dialing room service. That's not leadership.

It's a major misconception to imagine that successful implementation depends only on developing a brilliant description of the desired future state; that if we can just make that description vivid enough and express enough dissatisfaction with where we are now, the organization will march along on its own. The key to success in leading change is to understand that you are not just conceiving and describing an end point: You are leading the organization on a *journey* from its present state to a more desirable future state (Figure 6.2).

Implementation is all about the journey, and as a leader you have to shepherd the organization through the journey. That journey is filled with difficulties, pitfalls, and psychological stresses. It's never smooth sailing. And most often, it is a multiyear endeavor requiring staying power and relentless pursuit of what works and relentless pruning of what doesn't. Everyone in the organization needs to understand the realities of this journey, where they are at any given time, where each person fits into the overall effort, and what is expected of them. A sage once described leadership as the ability to create a compelling vision plus a practical method for

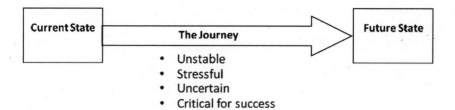

Figure 6.2   Change Leadership: A Journey to the Future

reaching it. It is not enough for employees to believe in the vision. They must also believe in the things that will get them there.

The Golden Rules of Successful Execution

Much has been written about the keys to successful execution. Psychologists emphasize the motivational elements; experts in operations point out the need for effective project management; organizational behaviorists focus on such issues as organizational design, reward mechanisms, and corporate culture; and strategists tend to stress the need for a clear direction, competitive advantage, and the right priorities. All these experts are right. All these things matter. But none of them works in isolation.

The work of leaders is integrative: They orchestrate the *right combination of things in the right alignment*. The power of alignment is like the difference between laser light and ordinary light. Ordinary light—tellingly called "incoherent light" in scientific parlance—is a diffuse scattering of all colors of the spectrum; laser light is a focused, powerful tool. Similarly, without the effective alignment of your whole organization behind your strategy, that strategy is sure to fail. But when your organization is correctly aligned behind the right strategy, its force is irresistible.

The best thinking in all the areas of effective execution can be synthesized into a list of four golden rules that will enable you to successfully navigate your journey and reach your destination. From my personal observations and all the research I have examined, my confidence in these golden rules is very high—so high, in fact, that I am prepared to stick my neck out and offer a guarantee: If you do not follow these simple rules, your change effort will falter or fail.

But it is also a perverse guarantee. Even if you *do* follow these rules, no matter how diligently, there is no absolute guarantee of success. Business is a game of risk and probabilities. So the key is to avoid the guarantee of failure and to push the favorable probabilities as high as you can. Ultimate success is a matter of leadership

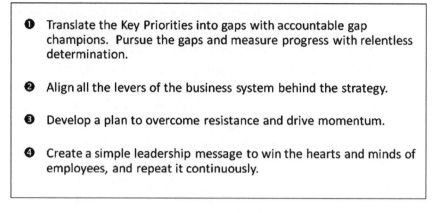

❶ Translate the Key Priorities into gaps with accountable gap champions. Pursue the gaps and measure progress with relentless determination.

❷ Align all the levers of the business system behind the strategy.

❸ Develop a plan to overcome resistance and drive momentum.

❹ Create a simple leadership message to win the hearts and minds of employees, and repeat it continuously.

Figure 6.3 Keys to Successful Implementation

capability. That's why I can't give you a guarantee of success; only you can guarantee your own leadership effectiveness.

The golden rules are presented in Figure 6.3.

We'll examine golden rules 1 and 2 in this chapter. In Chapter 7, we'll take on golden rule 3, and in Chapter 8, we will look into rule 4. Just remember: To achieve success, all four rules must be applied as an integrated and mutually reinforcing process.

Let's start with golden rule 1.

Closing the Gaps

Every leader asks the same question when they're going through the alignment journey: How can I get the organization to do what I want it to do?

The key is to understand that success happens twice: first in your mind and then in the field of action. The vision of success has to crystallize in your mind and in the minds of everyone in the organization before you can expect it to materialize externally.

Priorities are somewhat static, a statement of the few things that are most important. The magic of excelling is to understand what brilliant success looks like for each priority. You take the first step toward success by visualizing what that brilliant success looks like in very specific, concrete ways. You can smell it, you can taste it. Only then can you expect to accomplish it in reality.

I remember as a schoolboy being fascinated by the challenge of breaking the four-minute mile. Many people thought it was impossible, because there is an undeniable limit to what human beings can achieve. "After all," I remember one prominent figure saying, "it's totally impossible for a human to run a mile in one minute, so maybe we've reached that limit with the four-minute barrier." And for years, these pundits were right.

Then a magic thing happened on May 6, 1954, at the Iffley Road running track in Oxford, England. Roger Bannister made history by running one mile in 3 minutes, 59.4 seconds. Even more important, when he powered past the timer, Bannister broke through the wall of doubt and disbelief. "There was a mystique, a belief that it couldn't be done," Bannister recalled more than 50 years later. "But I think it was more of a psychological barrier than a physical barrier."

He was absolutely right. Australian John Landy, one of the best milers of that time, had never gotten closer to the 4-minute mark than 1.5 seconds. But just 46 days later, he, too, broke the barrier with a time of 3 minutes, 57.9 seconds. By the end of 1957, 16 runners had logged subfour-minute miles. The only thing that changed: They knew they could.

Once this happened, the whole conversation changed. I remember someone saying, "Why are people running faster than before?" The answer is in Virgil, the classical Roman poet: We can because we think we can.

If you think about this in the context of gaps that define success, after Bannister's great feat, John Landy defined success at 1.5 seconds faster than he had run up to that point. Once he had the vision in his head that it was possible, he went on to achieve it.

The Key Priorities described in Chapter 5 mobilize Pareto's relentless 80/20 principle. They define the vital few things that will make the biggest difference to the achievement of the Winning Proposition. They ensure concentrated effort—that the large wheel at the top will set all the smaller wheels spinning on the right things.

But for these priorities to energize the organization and move it ahead on its journey to excellence, each one must be translated into a gap statement describing how to complete the journey to the

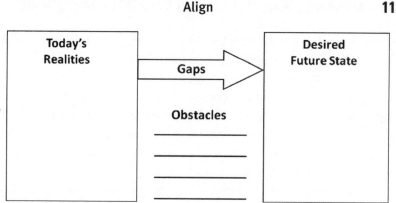

Figure 6.4 Defining Gaps

desired future state. Each gap statement should have a clear starting point, milestones, and a vivid picture of success, as illustrated in Figure 6.4.

Our job is to ask ourselves, "How do we stretch to even greater levels?" I encourage you to be bold and ambitious when you define your gaps, just as John Landy did when he understood what was possible.

Begin by designating a gap champion to be responsible for each priority. The gap champion should head up a cross-functional gap team of four to six people whose goal is to convert their assigned priority into a gap statement: They have to clarify the gaps that must be closed for that priority to be achieved, then work together cohesively as a task force, and take full responsibility for success.

For this gap-closing process to achieve its full potential, the gap champions must be executives with drive, imagination, and enthusiasm; and they must be able to bring others along with them. This is not a bureaucratic role focused on incrementalism. It is often about breaking with the past and creating new pathways to excellence.

The gap teams should be asked to accept full accountability for closing the gaps assigned to them. But there is a reciprocal side to this bargain. Gap champions must have the right to ask the organization for help or resources to overcome obstacles, and the organization must unfailingly be willing to provide these. This will ensure the organization unfailingly dedicates the necessary energy and resources to the few things that matter most.

For gap statements to be meaningful, they must include a cold-eyed description of the current state. Current realities are not always obvious to everyone, and are prone to wishful thinking, evasions, political correctness, and all those elements that play tricks on our objectivity. Unless these realities are spelled out rigorously, the necessary changes will not be clear.

After clarifying the current state, the gap teams should define the desired future state as the next step. It will not be easy to identify what stands in the way until the end point has been clarified. And in any event, focusing on obstacles at this intermediate point will tend to limit the ambition of what is possible.

Once the desired future state has been described, it is necessary to lay out the main obstacles that must be overcome along the way. This helps everyone understand the realities of the journey and what it will take to succeed.

One final point about the gap-closing process: I recommend that at every formal business review, the first item on the agenda should be a progress report by the gap champions. Symbolically, the first item on an agenda is regarded as the most important one. Placing this first underscores the fact that nothing is more important than achieving the desired future state on each of the Strategic Priorities. This will keep the organization's strategic focus constantly in the spotlight, create a transparent way to measure progress, promote a discussion on how to remove obstacles, and provide an opportunity to celebrate successes. The result is that everyone feels they are part of the journey.

For example, the Girl Scouts assigned Julie Murphy, the senior director of strategy, to coordinate the gaps process. She held regular meetings with the gap champions to streamline the work, cross-fertilize best practices, agree on sequencing, manage resource allocation, and ensure that timelines were being adhered to. Regular progress meetings were also held with the CEO.

Following are examples of the gap statements defined by the Girl Scouts. They are built from the Key Priorities shown on page 117. At the top of each gap statement is the specific priority that it addresses.

Priority: Build the world's best integrated leadership development system that defines activities and outcomes differentiated by age level for girls 5 to 17 (Figure 6.5).

Gaps

CURRENT STATE	FUTURE STATE	OBSTACLES
There is a myriad activities but no clear definition of the essential elements of Girl Scouts. Girl experiences are inconsistent, with no clear outcome measures.	There is a consistent Girl Scouts experience centered on a powerful model of leadership development, which is tied to clear outcome measures.	Balancing girl desires for fun and variety with the organizational need for focus. Pressure to develop activities in response to funding opportunities.
Existing age levels are inconsistent with girl needs and development. Language and symbols of belonging are outdated.	Age levels provide girls with appropriate opportunities to progress. Language and symbols of belonging are relevant and contemporary.	There is an unhealthy devotion to traditions on standards, uniforms, and awards.
Community service has declined as a core program element and is not leveraged as a key differentiator.	The power of girls together is galvanized around community service projects that make a difference.	Adults lack information to coach girls on powerful community service campaigns.

Figure 6.5 Build World's Best Leadership Development System

Priority: Develop a state-of-the-art model of volunteerism whereby volunteers can qualify easily and serve in flexible ways (Figure 6.6).

Gaps

CURRENT STATE	FUTURE STATE	OBSTACLES
Recruitment of volunteers overburdens parents of elementary school girls. Screening procedures are inconsistent.	Recruitment mobilizes a diversity of adults who are able to join easily and commit to serving the Girl Scouts mission.	Inexperience with volunteer recruitment and a culture that is unwelcoming to "others" contribute to maintenance of the status quo.
Adults who volunteer are engaged in preparatory steps that are outdated and fail to address time constraints and busy lives.	Continuous, state-of-the-art learning programs prepare volunteers for flexible service.	Some staff and volunteers serve as gatekeepers for longstanding traditions and practices related to "training."

Figure 6.6 Develop State-of-the Art Volunteerism Model

Priority: Substantially increase contributed income to fund a vibrant Girl Scouts movement (Figure 6.7).

Gaps

CURRENT STATE	FUTURE STATE	OBSTACLES
Internal sources of income are inadequate to fund the new program at a high level of excellence.	Contributed income enables the new program model to perform to its full potential.	Culture that prides itself on "making do" with very little. Inexperience and fear related to raising contributed income.
Historic overreliance on internal sources of revenue has allowed us to neglect efforts to raise contributed income up to this point.	A dynamic external focus fuels contributed income streams. National and council leadership make fundraising a true priority.	There is sometimes denial and resistance around the need to raise contributed income. There is complacency with current funding patterns. Staff and volunteer skill and experience levels are often inadequate.
There is no movementwide, strategic, and coordinated plan for raising contributed income.	An integrated national fund-raising strategy based on the new program model exponentially increases contributed income. There is widespread understanding of a compelling case for supporting Girl Scouts.	Cultural issues include: turf, protectionism, mistrust, and silos. The external public does not know or understand the case for supporting Girl Scouts.

Figure 6.7 Substantially Increase Contributed Income

Priority: Transform the Girl Scouts image with a compelling, contemporary brand that inspires girls of every culture to join (Figure 6.8).

Gaps

CURRENT STATE	FUTURE STATE	OBSTACLES
"High brand recognition" does not result in perception of Girl Scouts as relevant, appealing, and of the moment. There is no clearly defined focus.	Girls are attracted by a national brand that focuses on the impact of the updated program model on girls' lives. Girl Scouts is the organization of choice for girls 5 to 17 of every culture.	Diffused brand development efforts with myriad special initiatives. Dedication to tradition inhibits creation of a unified, relevant image.
Adult members do not view themselves as brand champions and are generally not prepared to take on this role.	Staff and volunteers at all levels of the organization model the brand by striving to "live" the mission, promise/law.	A "do it my way" sense of entitlement contributes to the perpetuation of negative images.

Figure 6.8 Transform Girl Scouts Brand Image

Priority: Create an effective organizational structure and democratic governance system that achieves decisiveness, speed of action, and best use of resources (Figure 6.9).

Gaps

CURRENT STATE	FUTURE STATE	OBSTACLES
The national and local governance systems are slow and overly reliant on "Robert's Rules" and consensus building.	Girl Scouts is governed by an efficient democratic system that moves quickly from discussion to decision and alignment. The movement keeps pace with real-time issues.	There is a lack of trust in decision makers and a propensity to overvalue discussion and undervalue action.
There are 315 councils whose capacities vary widely. This challenges the resources of the movement. There is ambiguity about the role and value of the national organization.	Efficient councils, accountable to clear performance standards, deliver consistent, high-quality Girl Scout experiences. The GSUSA role is valued and understood.	There is disagreement about performance standards and courses of action when standards are not met.

Figure 6.9   Create Effective Organization and Governance System

The Business Ecosystem

We move now to the second golden rule for successful implementation: *Align all the levers of your business system behind your strategy.*

Getting the gap teams working productively is essential for success. But it is not enough. Achieving effective business system alignment is a crucial additional requirement.

When implementing a new strategy, organizations often fall into what I call the MTI (managing things in isolation) trap. This happens when they conclude that changing just one thing in their business system will independently make all the difference between success and failure. Changing the organization structure is a favorite. Changing the incentive system and announcing a new set of organizational values are also popular.

So what's wrong with initiatives like these? Nothing, per se. The real problem is that none of them is likely to work in isolation. For any strategy to succeed, it is necessary for *all* the key elements of an organization's business system to be aligned synergistically in support of that strategy and in mutual support of each other. This requires systems thinking, the ability to understand and mobilize your business system in a holistic way.

The key is to think about your business system as an ecosystem. The hallmark of an ecosystem is mutual interdependence. Ecosystems are formed and will thrive based on a strong process of mutual support between their key components. When any one of those components fails to play this supporting role, the ecosystem will fail.

For example, in the human body—to cite a complex ecosystem everyone is intimately familiar with—each organ and each subsystem has a unique role, but none can work in isolation. Each contributes to the success of the other and makes our total biological ecosystem function to its full potential. If one subsystem—whether it's the nervous system, skeletal, digestive, or circulatory system—underperforms, the effectiveness of the whole body is undermined, regardless of how well the others perform. We don't usually think about this intricate web of finely tuned interrelationships and how they help sustain our overall state of health and vitality until one goes awry. Then we diagnose which body part is ailing. Fixing it leads to overall wellness.

Every organization succeeds or fails according to those very same principles of mutual interdependence. A symphony orchestra produces wonderful music not because of the actions of any one individual but as a result of the well-coordinated work of the entire group. Otherwise, it would produce cacophony. Similarly, for a company to be successful, all of its interdependent parts must operate in sync with one another and with the firm's strategy. Success comes not from isolated actions but from orchestrating the right *inter*actions.

In the Align step of the Strategic Learning cycle, the basic components of a business system—Measures and Rewards, Structure and Process, Culture and People—are all connected (Figure 6.10).

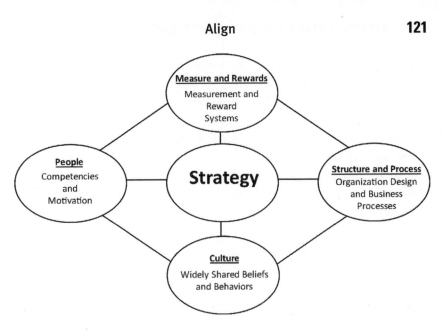

Figure 6.10 Aligning the Business System

I have placed strategy at the center of the illustration to remind us that the entire purpose of a business system is to support the strategy. The starting point for achieving effective business system alignment is to place the Winning Proposition and Key Priorities center stage, then pose this question: "How will we align each component of our business system so that it supports our strategy?"

The chances are that your existing alignment system was built up through various adjustments over time to attain a tighter and tighter alignment behind your *old* strategy. It is very unlikely that this existing alignment system will automatically support a significantly changed strategy. What's more likely is that it may well work *against* the new strategy, and these impediments could prove crippling. Without effective business system realignment, you could end up sabotaging your own strategy.

Organizations often tackle these realignments piecemeal. As they strive to implement new strategies, they run into obstacles caused by misalignments in one component or another, and then apply fixes over time. The realignment process drags out and strategy implementation slows down or stalls. The way to avoid this is to realign the total system, as an integrated system, behind the strategy from the outset. The big payoff is that your business system will then be working at full power, helping to drive your strategy forward.

As an example of how an alignment system will vary based on the strategic goals of an organization, let's compare two hypothetical alternatives: an organization whose main emphasis is on manufacturing efficiency versus an organization whose strategy is focused on product innovation. Let's assume the former is an oil refinery and the latter is in the snack foods business. Notice how the difference in their basic strategies dictates differences in every aspect of their business systems (Figure 6.11).

Now, as a mind experiment, swap the two business systems around, and ask yourself whether either of these two businesses could succeed if it inherited the other organization's alignment system. This idea would be clearly absurd. Of course, this example represents two polarized extremes. Few organizations would fit into a totally rigid mold. An oil refinery would probably have an R&D department working on process innovation, and a snack food company would need to run its production lines efficiently. There is no "one size fits all" business system that we can order off the shelf. Each alignment system needs to be deeply customized to what the particular organization is aiming to achieve.

	ABC Oil Refinery (Efficiency Organization)	XYZ Snack Foods (Innovation Organization)
Measures and Rewards	Focused mainly on operational excellence and improving efficiencies.	Focused mainly on customer generation and retention and the creation of new products.
Structure and Processes	More formal structures, strict protocols, and centralized controls; often organized by product line or function.	Fewer controls, decentralized structures, venturing units; often organized by customer grouping.
Culture	Emphasis on continuous improvement and embedding what works.	Emphasis on risk-taking, experimentation, and challenging the status quo.
People	Emphasis on professional/functional rigor; greater continuity of job tenure.	More free thinkers and mavericks; greater job rotation.

Figure 6.11 Efficiency versus Innovation Organization

The way to create effective alignment is to examine each component of the business ecosystem and ask these two questions:

▼ How will this particular component support the strategy we are pursuing?

▼ How will this component help the other components do the same job?

The result you want is that each element will directly support the strategy, and all of them will work synergistically together toward that end.

Alignment in Action

Here's an increasingly common challenge: As more intense competition demands that companies move up the hierarchy of customer needs, many companies are making the transition from selling only products to selling products combined with services in order to create integrated solutions for their customers. As discussed in Chapter 5, Sysco is such an example. Other examples are IBM (about half its business is now in services), Ericsson, and Henry Schein, Inc., the dental/medical products distribution company. The business systems of these companies would originally have been designed with the sole purpose of selling products profitably. How would these companies have needed to realign their business systems (ecosystems) to excel at the new solutions-based strategy? Here are some of the important adjustments that would have been necessary.

Measures and Rewards. The new system would require measures and rewards for the delivery of integrated customer solutions. The performance of customer service teams would become just as important as manufacturing productivity.

Structure and Process. Organization design would need to include structures for managing and deploying service teams. R&D would have to embrace both product and service innovation. Perhaps most important would be understanding that the consumption of a service is not an event, but a process. Therefore, a business model would be required to deliver solutions that provide a superior end-to-end customer experience.

Culture. Collaboration and teamwork combined with rapid responsiveness to the needs of customers would be vital elements of the culture.

People. The new competency model would need to incorporate skills in service excellence, teamwork, and the creation of innovative customer solutions.

This may seem pretty mundane, but that's the nature of an ecosystem that's running well, with all of its components working together in mutual support. You hardly pay it much attention. But if you don't pull them together in a holistic way, this will result in underperformance or even failure.

There are, of course, situations where not all the components of the business system need to change to support a new strategy. In that case, the best approach is to make the changes by exception. Examine each component and ask, "Is there a misalignment here we need to correct?" If nothing (or very little) needs to change in a particular lever of the system, move on to the next element and make only the changes that are necessary to ensure total system alignment. The key is the mental discipline of systems thinking, and orchestrating the right combination of things. When aligning your business system, don't think actions, think *interactions*.

The Importance of the "Soft Stuff"

Are some components of a business system harder to change than others? The answer is definitely yes.

Think of Measures and Rewards and Structure and Process as the "hardware" of your business system and Culture and People as its "software." The hardware and software need to work together in a process of mutual support. In pulling that off, experience has shown that modifying the software is much more challenging than changing the hardware. That's because the software involves the skills, attitudes, and behaviors of people.

Changing the measurement system or altering the organizational design, for example, can be implemented quite quickly. It might take the employees a short while to adjust to these changes, but they will soon become the norm. It is an altogether different matter to change the culture, competencies, or basic motivations in the organization. These are not simply events or short projects; they involve ongoing campaigns.

The main thing to remember is this: Just as an ecosystem cannot survive without the support of all of its components, so an organization needs to effectively align both the hard stuff and the soft stuff in order to excel. And mostly the soft stuff is what trips you up. Almost invariably, when organizations change their strategy in a major way, they're confronted with the hard task of changing their culture.

Changing an Organization's Culture

The most widely misunderstood part of an organization's business system is its culture, yet it is arguably the most powerful lever of all. Culture is often the biggest barrier to change, the hardest one to deal with, and, far too frequently, the most overlooked. This gives us a special reason to emphasize its role in alignment.

The key to success in changing a corporate culture is a clear understanding of what culture is. A quick definition:

Culture refers to the values we deem to be important, and the accompanying behaviors we expect of ourselves and each other.

How do you know what an organization's culture is? By observing its behaviors. These behaviors persist because they are rewarded and because failure to practice them is penalized.

A society's culture develops as a way of solving the problems it faces, including economic problems (How will we distribute resources among the members of our society?); political problems (How will important decisions affecting the members of our society be made?); and social problems (How will conflicts between groups in our society be resolved?). Like nations, not-for-profit organizations and commercial enterprises all have their own cultures, which are also problem-solving mechanisms: a means to an end rather than an end in themselves.

Culture-building is all about inculcating shared beliefs and behaviors. But influencing behavior is a tough thing to do. Because culture is the manifestation of the behavior of an entire group, it's not something that can be fractionalized.

Often in my executive seminars I pose this question: "If your culture conflicts with your strategy, which one will win: your culture or your strategy?" Invariably the participants reply in a unified chorus: "Culture will win every time!" I then ask if they can cite any exceptions, and no one can. The conclusion: If your strategy and your culture are misaligned, you are in big trouble.

We don't have to go far to find examples. Let's revisit the General Motors meltdown for a moment. No one would make the argument that GM's executives were lacking in intelligence. They no doubt recruited the best brains they could find. We can be certain that their analytical skills were first-rate.

The heart of GM's problem was an inward-looking, bureaucratic culture wedded to repeating the past rather than inventing the future. Hubris about past successes led to a state of denial that their problems were life-threatening. Over time, they grew more and more out of touch with their customers. Without a fix to that adverse culture, GM was facing formidable headwinds (and will continue to face them now that it has emerged from Chapter 11). I'm not suggesting that those at the top were not aware of this problem, nor that they didn't try to change the culture. What is clear, however, is that they haven't yet succeeded in doing so. What is equally clear is that a change in the culture was and will remain a necessary condition for success in turning the company around. At a news conference following GM's exit from bankruptcy protection, former Chief Executive Frederick Henderson said, "Our culture to this point has been an impediment. . . . Business as usual is over at GM. Everyone at GM must realize this and be prepared to change, and fast."[1]

Does the GM experience prove that culture change in large, complex organizations is impossible? The evidence does not support such a conclusion. Look at Lou Gerstner's remarkable turnaround of a collapsing IBM in the mid-1990s, described in his book,

Who Says Elephants Can't Dance? Inside IBM's Historic Turn-around (HarperCollins Publishers Inc., 2002). What Gerstner, who was hired from the outside, recognized at the outset was that culture change was going to be the first order of business after clarifying the company's strategic focus. He quickly figured out with the IBM team what the business strategy was going to be, and then immediately set about changing the culture to support that strategy. He recognized that a culture/strategy misalignment would be fatal to the turnaround. He said: "Fixing the corporate culture is the most critical—and most difficult—part of a corporate transformation."

It can be argued that large-scale culture change requires the appointment of a leader from the outside, that insiders are really too much part of the history and the current mind-sets. I think that's too narrow a view. I would argue that the real challenge is for the leadership to understand the power of culture and to successfully harness that power in support of the organization's strategy. There is no reason why an insider cannot do that.

This is exactly what Girl Scouts CEO Kathy Cloninger set out to do. Kathy came up through the ranks of Girl Scouts (she had herself been a council CEO), but was completely clear on the need for culture change to support the new strategy. Her motto was, "The status quo has got to go."

The result was a new culture statement for the Girl Scouts, shown in Figure 6.12, which is expressed in terms of the behaviors they would hold themselves and their colleagues accountable for.

What makes their organizational challenge especially difficult is that each of the Girl Scouts councils is a legally separate entity, which makes the Girl Scouts more of a movement than a formally integrated structure. This is a challenge faced by almost all not-for-profit organizations, as well as many for-profit enterprises with multiple legacy businesses. The different entities have to work together cohesively with a shared purpose, because neither the organizational design alone nor the system of measures and rewards alone will carry them there. People have to enlist. Their commitment to a common set of values serves as both the glue and the dynamo that ultimately builds a high-performance culture, which, in turn, will drive success.

Girl-Centered
Girls are at the center of everything we do.

Inclusive
We build and maintain an environment in which diversity is represented and valued.

Aligned
We are interdependent and collaborative across all teams and *the Movement*.
We are empowered. We take risks to fulfill our mission to serve girls.

Accountable
We hold ourselves and each other responsible for our work and relationships.
We are committed to excellence. We are honest, trustworthy, and respectful.

Innovative
We are creative, innovative, learn continuously, and have fun together.

This is who we are.

Figure 6.12   The Girl Scout Culture—Our Ways of Behaving

Culture is the strongest thing you've got going for you, and it's the biggest impediment if you don't. That was what Gerstner found at IBM. When you fix the culture, everything else works better.

Measuring Culture

There's a widespread perception that organizational culture is vague and unmanageable. The opposite is true: It is specific, definable, measurable, and manageable.

How do you measure culture? There are many assessment tools offered by various consultants. In my view, most are too complicated, involving hundreds of questions that don't even tangentially refer to your culture statements.

I prefer a simpler instrument, with a straightforward five-point rating system. Figure 6.13 provides an example.

As you go through the questions based on your own culture statement, it's best to ask employees for two perspectives: a rating for the entire organization, regardless of which department the employee works in, and a rating for the employee's specific department or geographic region. The advantage is that this gives you a clear understanding of where the gaps are. And since the whole

Rating Scale:

Not At All	Limited Extent	Moderate Extent	Considerable Extent	Great Extent
1	2	3	4	5

Sample Questions:
- Are prudent risk-taking and experimentation encouraged at ABC?
- Do ABC's people help each other succeed through teamwork?
- Do people exhibit candor and trust at ABC?
- Is knowledge sharing practiced throughout ABC?

Figure 6.13   Measurement of Culture

point of measurement is to gauge progress, and since your goal is to achieve a rating of 5, you shouldn't just measure once. It is important to measure regularly—say once a year. (The measurements should be done by an independent research firm.) If, for example, a region or department scores 3 on certain items, that's the signal to hold a gaps workshop and decide which actions to take to close the gaps. Then when you next measure, you will be able to assess progress. Be sure to publicize the results. After all, you wouldn't keep the organization's cash flow a secret. Culture is an equally fundamental performance issue.

The point to remember is this: What you measure gets done, and what you reward gets done repeatedly. This rule applies to cash flow, to operational efficiency, and also to creating a high-performance culture.

Defining a High-Performance Culture

There is no more important leadership task than building a high-performance organizational culture. But what exactly is a high-performance culture? In my work with various organizations, I have begun to notice a common pattern. Almost always, after the new strategy has been defined, the nature of the necessary culture change covers some or all of the behaviors shown in Figure 6.14.

From		To
Conservative/complacent	→	Risk-taking and experimental
Slow/bureaucratic	→	Flexible and fast
Efficiency focused	→	Innovation focused
Product focused (inside-out)	→	Customer focused (outside-in)
Silos and fiefdoms	→	Acting in common interest
Knowledge hoarding	→	Sharing best practices

Figure 6.14   Achieving Cultural Transformation

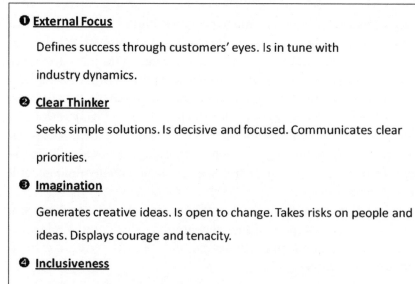

❶ External Focus

Defines success through customers' eyes. Is in tune with

industry dynamics.

❷ Clear Thinker

Seeks simple solutions. Is decisive and focused. Communicates clear

priorities.

❸ Imagination

Generates creative ideas. Is open to change. Takes risks on people and

ideas. Displays courage and tenacity.

❹ Inclusiveness

Is a team player. Respects others' ideas and contributions. Creates

engagement, builds loyalty, and commitment.

❺ Expertise

Has in-depth domain knowledge. Continuously develops self. Loves

learning.

Figure 6.15   GE Values

The pattern is very clear. A high-performance culture is an adaptive culture, finely tuned to the external environment and needs of customers, open to learning and knowledge-sharing, and one that acts with a sense of urgency. It is also invariably a culture of candor and trust. There may be some specific behaviors that will support a given strategy (such as providing integrated solutions for customers) but these adaptive behaviors are the keys to long-term success.

As an example, let's look at the culture of GE. Figure 6.15 shows the GE statement of its values.[2]

GE has described its culture in terms of shared behaviors, in simple, clear words that everyone can understand. There are no more than five of them. It is notable that these behaviors are based on learning and adaptation. And GE holds everyone accountable, through its measurement and reward systems, for living up to the values.

I have spent a good deal of time on the key issue of culture, because I believe it goes to the essence of effective leadership. Quoting Lou Gerstner again, "If the CEO isn't living and preaching the culture, and isn't doing it consistently, then it just doesn't happen."[3]

I would add this simple rider: Gerstner's statement applies to leaders at every level in the organization, whether you are leading a large division, a manufacturing plant, or a small team. If you don't manage the culture, it will manage you. And you can't delegate culture. As a leader, you *are* the culture.

Avoiding the Values Trap

Executives often proudly proclaim, "Our values will never change." But the problem is that if your strategy shifts and your culture remains static and out of sync with your strategy, your organization will falter or fail.

So much, then, for enduring values? Not exactly. I'd like to make a distinction between two crucial definitions, between *core values* and *instrumental values*.

Core values involve matters of principle. They produce behaviors that provide a moral compass (e.g., ethical standards, truthfulness, nondiscrimination, fairness, mutual respect, etc.) They should never change, and *must* never change. After all, you don't change your morality or your ethics. So to have any meaning, core values must be steadfast.

Then there are instrumental values. These are morally neutral. They produce behaviors essential to the success of the chosen strategy (e.g., customer-focused decision making, speed of action, operational discipline, knowledge-sharing, prudent risk-taking, etc.) There's nothing moral or immoral about speed of action or operational discipline. The only issue is whether these values promote behaviors that are aligned with your strategy.

When your strategy shifts, it is necessary to reexamine your instrumental values, not your core values. When managers say, "Our values will never change," they've made the mistake of melding the two together, and in doing so, they've frozen the whole lot. Now their organization's values are out of sync with its strategy, and that spells trouble.

GE analyzed what it would take to succeed in the new competitive environment and refreshed its instrumental values accordingly. The list of its new values is almost identical to the high-performance list in Figure 6.14. Significantly, the company's leadership has emphasized that living by these shared values will be crucial to the future success of the business and will therefore be expected of everyone. Clearly, those who do not put these values into practice will not flourish in GE.

In this chapter we've dealt with two of the four golden rules for effective implementation:

▼ Translate your Key Priorities into gaps, and appoint accountable gap champions.

▼ Align all the levers of your business system behind your strategy.

But resistance to change is as inevitable as the need to respond to change is inexorable. How, then, can leaders close the gap between these two opposing forces? That is the challenge we will address in the next chapter.

Overcoming Resistance to Change and Driving Momentum

I'm all for progress. It's change I object to.

—Mark Twain

n the Introduction to this book, I noted that one of the most important lessons I've learned over the years is never to underestimate the human element in strategy creation and implementation. It is, I said—and it's worth repeating—*the* governing factor in the success or failure of any organization.

Whenever I think about the human factor, I recall the time when I was president of Sterling Winthrop's global Consumer Health

Group. Our head of Human Resources was a very matter-of-fact, task-oriented man called Kyle Greer. Kyle had previously been a successful operations executive and was able to combine high efficiency with deep people sensitivity in his new role. If you wanted something on the HR front to be done effectively but without a nasty backlash, Kyle would take care of it. On one occasion, I was so impressed with how he had dealt with a particularly thorny task that I bounded into his office to express my gratitude and admiration. "Kyle, you are an ace at this HR role," I said. "Tell me, do you enjoy running the HR function?" Kyle replied, "Yes, if it wasn't for the people!"

Kyle was only half joking. What caused him the most agony was dealing with all the complex psychological and emotional factors that make us human: the turf battles, the need for recognition, career disappointment, self-doubt, status anxiety, and, above all, resistance to change.

In Chapter 6, we covered the first two of the four golden rules for successful implementation of a strategy. If you have followed these, you will have:

▼ Mobilized gap teams, led by energetic gap champions, to close the gaps on each key priority.

▼ Ensured that all the levers of your business system are powerfully aligned in support of your strategy.

With these two elements in place, you have now taken care of some of the crucial factors for success—but not all of them. Therefore, you cannot yet expect to see quick or fully effective results. There is still a major roadblock in your way: the natural tendency of human beings to resist change. In the Strategic Learning process, we're now at the crux of the Align step: dealing with people (see Figure 7.1).

That's why the third golden rule is: *Develop a plan to overcome resistance and drive momentum.*

Any new strategy invariably involves change, and being an adaptive enterprise means dealing with change as a way of life. Sometimes these are small adjustments; other times, more radical shifts

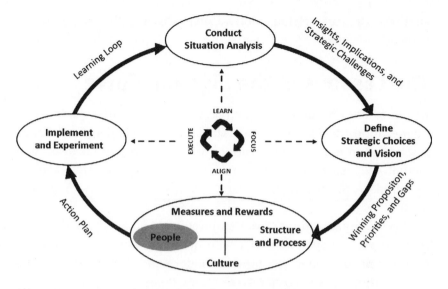

Figure 7.1 Leading through Strategic Learning: Align

are required. It is never true that everything needs to change. But it is also never true that nothing needs to change. An organization never "arrives." It is always becoming.

Dealing with the Sources of Resistance

Leading change is not just an intellectual task of understanding what needs to be done, explaining what needs to be done, and then expecting it to be done. As Kyle Greer discovered, effective leadership of change requires the ability to tune into and effectively deal with the concerns, needs, and expectations of the people in the organization.

However, people are often themselves unaware of their underlying biases and fears. The opposition to change won't be expressed in emotional or psychological terms. You will seldom hear people say, "I feel threatened by that change," or "I have a hard time coping with uncertainty." These emotions will be rationalized into business arguments. The causes of resistance will most often be emotional, but the ammunition employed will be intellectual. The vital skill is the ability to "read" the organization and understand the emotional subtext—the underlying motivations—driving the oppositional behavior.

The Lessons of the Sigmoid Curve

Evidence shows that the single biggest cause of failure is the way organizations deal with success. That's why the challenge of change is greatest in mature organizations with a history of success. Will Durant, the historian, summed it up well: "Great civilizations are not defeated from the outside. They destroy themselves from the inside."[1]

Social organizations, from empires to businesses to nonprofit enterprises, largely adhere to a set of inherent natural laws. To successfully lead change, we need to understand these laws and the barriers they create in order to overcome them.

Without a source of renewal, the life of organizations, like biological life, is self-limiting. Generally, after surmounting the initial struggle to get started, an organization gains momentum and a period of growth (phase one) ensues, followed by deepening maturity (phase two), decline and eventual death (phase three). This tendency is illustrated by the sigmoid curve shown in Figure 7.2.[2] The initial downward curve denotes the start-up challenges of fighting the odds and spending more resources than you are earning.

Think about some of the great empires in history: the Mongolian, Greek, Spanish, Portuguese, British, and, more recently, the Soviet empire. Every single one went through a cycle of growth, maturity,

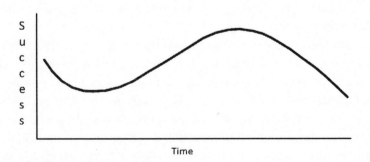

Figure 7.2 The Sigmoid Curve

stagnation, and demise. Some had long life cycles, others shorter ones, but all came to an end.

The business world is replete with similar examples. As I mentioned in Chapter 1, the number of new companies in the Fortune Top 20 increased from 35 percent in the decade ending in 1983 to 60 percent in the decade that ended in 2003. Some fell from grace quickly, like Enron, while others suffered a slow decline, like General Motors.

Why does this happen? Is it inevitable, like the biological cycle of life and death? Or can social organizations like companies defy these forces? After all, there are companies like ExxonMobil, Procter & Gamble, and GE that are well over 100 years old and still going strong.

The answer to these questions can be found within the two inescapable lessons of the sigmoid curve:

▼ Nothing lasts forever under its original momentum.

▼ Success contains the seeds of its own destruction.

These two rules are as powerful as the law of gravity.

The Curse of Success

To understand how these rules operate, we need to explore what goes on in the attitudes and behaviors within organizations as they evolve through the first two critical stages of the sigmoid curve, as depicted by Figure 7.3.

> *Phase one: Growth and discovery.* After organizations have experienced a successful birth, a growth phase ensues. The major preoccupation is to generate and retain customers. The keys to ongoing success have not yet been fully worked out, so there is a lot of experimentation and a zest for discovery and innovation. Speed and flexibility are hallmarks. At this stage, organizations are learning their way to success.
>
> *Phase two: Maturity and the curse of success.* When organizations reach the top of the sigmoid curve, they have attained

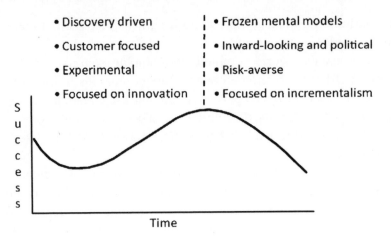

Figure 7.3 The Curse of Success

maturity. They are now well established, widely recognized as successful, and often large and complex. They feel they have figured out the keys to success.

Phase two is the stage of greatest danger. A set of symptoms begins to take hold, which represent barriers to successful change. Some of these symptoms are psychological, some organizational, and others cultural. Together, they amount to a malady often referred to as the curse of success. These are the seeds of an organization's own destruction. This condition, in the absence of a strong antidote, can turn into a debilitating and often fatal disease. Here are the most common symptoms of the curse of success: *trapped by frozen mental models, inward-looking and political, risk-averse,* and *focused on incrementalism.*

Trapped by Frozen Mental Models

When organizations have achieved notable success, they increasingly begin to believe that they, uniquely, understand what works and what doesn't. Past drivers of success become entrenched dogma for guiding the future. These underlying ideas can become subject to what psychologists call the confirmation bias, the tendency to selectively seek evidence to support these beliefs, and to reject any disconfirming evidence. Worst of all, any internal challenges to these convictions are regarded as disloyal. Such ingrained mental models are hard to escape. The psychologist Howard Gardner refers to them in his book *Changing Minds: The Art and Science of Changing Our Own and Other People's Minds* as "engravings in the brain," requiring a process of "mental bulldozing" to clear them out of the way and make room for reexamination.[3]

Assumptions drive decisions, and in time, these embedded assumptions get overtaken by events. Lew Platt, the former CEO of Hewlett-Packard, witnessed this pattern many times during his career in the fast-paced world of Silicon Valley. "I think of how easy it is to keep doing what you are doing today for a little bit too long," he said. "[Many] formerly successful companies did not make gigantic mistakes. The only real mistake they made was to keep doing what made them successful for a little too long."[4]

As I stated earlier, answers are dangerous until you have asked the right questions. To sustain life, organizations need a deliberate process to challenge their own assumptions. This is just as important as oxygen is to organic life.

Inward-Looking and Political

Mature companies become large, complicated, and difficult to run. Over time, an intense preoccupation develops about internal issues such as roles, responsibilities, reporting relationships, bureaucratic procedures, and organizational structures. This internal fixation begins to supersede concerns about industry trends, the needs of customers, and the actions of competitors.

Organizations are political systems. Inward-looking organizations amplify the influence of internal politics. The focus is on the enemy within. The company becomes rife with power struggles, self-interest maneuvers, favor exchanges, and all the rest. Taken to an extreme, these factors can become cripplingly dysfunctional.

The way I look at this, there are good politics and bad politics. Good politics involve campaigning behind ideas. Bad politics are focused on campaigning against people. Politically healthy organizations are outwardly focused. They understand that success flows from what you accomplish outside the organization, not inside.

Risk-averse and Focused on Incrementalism

Inward-focused organizations typically become risk-averse. Not only do they fail to heed the external forces that call for major change, but decisions are based on what's good for the careers, reputations, and financial welfare of the executives running the enterprise. The most senior people are often those closest to retirement. Keeping the existing policies going for the next quarter or the next 12 months is usually a safer bet for their personal interests than embarking on a risky new course. The resulting failure, as Lew Platt pointed out, often is not triggered by a cataclysmic event but by just continuing to do what you have been doing for a little bit too long.

A key indicator of this symptom is a fear of cannibalizing the existing business. Few organizations are able to muster the courage shown by Intel when it launched into microprocessors and totally displaced its own memory business. But then few are confronted by this all-or-nothing choice. Mostly, organizations need to renew themselves more progressively, by cannibalizing and renewing parts of their own business, piece by piece. However, the Parmenides Fallacy, which I described in Chapter 5, often overtakes the thinking, and organizations take refuge in the illusory safety of just hammering away at what they have been doing all along.

These are all symptoms of the same underlying disease. All mature organizations will tend to suffer from them to one degree or another. If the symptoms are left untreated, they will get worse. When this disease becomes advanced, these companies will have simply stopped learning. This can be a fatal condition. At that point, these organizations will have entered phase three.

Launching the Second Curve

It is important to understand the critical lessons of the sigmoid curve so we can devise ways to apply the necessary antidotes. The crucial leadership skill is a keen, unflinching sense of reality: the ability to diagnose and confront the underlying symptoms and act before it's too late. That's why the seven most dangerous words in the English language are, "If it ain't broke, don't fix it."

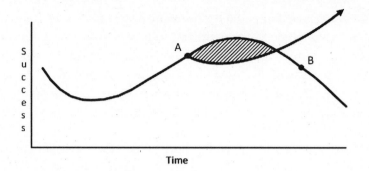

Figure 7.4   The Second Curve

Herein lies the final and most important lesson of the sigmoid curve: Launch the second curve while you are still successful. In other words, "If we don't fix it, it will break."

Organizations that achieve long-term success are able to initiate a series of sigmoid curves. They do not rely on past successes to carry them forward. They know that nothing lasts forever under its original momentum. But here's the key. In the second curve diagram, shown in Figure 7.4, the shaded area shows the critical time for change. Research shows unquestionably that the best time for a company to change is while it is still successful (soon after point A). Conversely, the worst time to try and launch a change is when a company is already in a state of decline (point B).

The world is dynamic, and that means competition is time-bound. You can't put your problems in the refrigerator and hope they will remain fresh. There is a window of time to act—*before* the market signals become a drumbeat of doom. Girl Scouts CEO Kathy Cloninger was galvanized when she saw how a gradual downward trend in membership became a rapid decline in Canada and Australia, threatening the very existence of the organization in those countries. She recognized a similar slow decline in the United States and realized that if left too long, the erosion of membership among early teens could turn into an irresistible downward spiral. General Motors, on the other hand, seemed to be frozen in the headlights, and ended up in a death march. No matter which industry you're in, your competitors will sense your hesitation and pounce on the opportunity.

The harsh reality is this: The highest probability of successful change exists while your organization is still successful, but that's exactly when the support for change is at its lowest. All the symptoms of the curse of success represent a formidable set of obstacles. The problem is that if you wait until you begin to fail, the support for change may well be stronger but the chances of success will be at their lowest.

Former GE chief Jack Welch said, "When the rate of change outside a company is greater than the rate of change inside a company, the end is near."[5] That discrepancy is especially prevalent in the context of a VUCA environment. It can be overcome by keeping in mind the lessons of the sigmoid curve.

These lessons go to the heart of successful leadership: the ability to create on organization capable of ongoing renewal.

McDonald's Shows How

During the 1990s, McDonald's, the popular hamburger chain, seemed to go into a funk as trendier competitors more in tune with evolving consumer tastes started cutting into the company's market share of fast foods. The onslaught gained momentum as McDonald's was increasingly denigrated for selling unhealthy, fat-laden food. It began to look as if this historic franchise may have had its day.

At first, McDonald's reaction was misguided. In an attempt to compensate for the threat to its market share, it embarked on a frenzied campaign of opening new restaurants—as many as 2,000 per year. With its focus diverted from the fundamentals, customer service and cleanliness began to deteriorate. Inevitably, same-store sales, the acid test of competitiveness, started to decline. At the beginning of 2003, McDonald's suffered its first quarterly loss in history, and the outlook seemed bleak.

But under the leadership first of James Cantalupo and then James Skinner, the company's current chief executive, McDonald's pulled off a remarkable turnaround. The springboard was a crucial shift in focus from adding more restaurants to creating greater customer value within existing restaurants—essentially moving up the hierarchy of customer needs. The company crystallized its new strategy in a simple, compelling one-page document called its "Plan to Win," which became a rallying point and source of inspiration for all its franchisees. The "Plan to Win" redefines what McDonald's stands for and clarifies its key priorities for success into what it calls the "five Ps": People, Products, Place, Price, and Promotion.

The five Ps were based on thorough research on what customers valued most. Guided by these insights, menus were updated to include healthy options such as salads and apple slices; McNuggets were changed to include only white meat; opening hours were extended to accommodate more breakfast and late-night customers; premium-quality coffee was introduced; restaurants were redecorated to provide a more pleasing atmosphere; and customer service and cleanliness returned to center stage. The company's mission was changed from "being the world's best quick-service restaurant" to being "our customers' favorite place and way to eat." As described by Andrew Martin in a *New York Times* article, "At McDonald's, the Happiest Meal Is Hot Profits" (January 11, 2009), "that shift in emphasis forced McDonald's employees to focus on quality, service, and restaurant experience rather than being the cheapest, most convenient option to customers."[6]

The results have been impressive. The volume decline has been reversed, and as of August 2009, the company had registered 63 consecutive months of increases in same store sales.[7]

The McDonald's implementation effectiveness is instructive for three reasons:

▼ The makeover was based on critical insights into the customer hierarchy of needs, as the company recognized that consumer patterns had changed and that McDonald's needed to adapt.

▼ Its "Plan to Win" was reduced to a simple one-page statement that everyone could readily understand. It was the perfect vehicle for organizational alignment throughout the entire franchise, which, notes CEO Skinner, has been a pivotal factor in McDonald's revival. Furthermore, the gaps between the company's unfavorable current state and desired future state were stark, clear, and actionable.

▼ Finally, McDonald's acted within its window of opportunity. When it picked up the negative signals, it promptly dived into a program of consumer research, did some early experiments to see what worked, found the right formula for success, and rolled out the new strategy before the negative momentum consumed it.

One other key lesson emerges from the McDonald's example. It reinforces a classical rule of strategy. The first order of business, whether it is a military strategy or a business strategy, is to protect and reinforce your base. Once your base falls apart, all else is lost. To begin with, McDonald's lost sight of this principle and chased new store openings while its base business deteriorated. To its credit, it realized this misstep and quickly corrected it. I like to summarize this key lesson with this maxim: *Strengthen the core, then go for more.*

Overcoming the sources of resistance and creating fresh momentum ensures that an organization starts moving in the new direction while it still has the resources to do so. The following actions have been shown to be powerful factors in successfully launching the second curve: *maximize participation, generate short-term wins, deal directly with resisters,* and *set a shining example.*

Maximize Participation

Charlotte Beers, the first female CEO of the worldwide advertising agency Ogilvy and Mather, estimated that at the outset of any major change initiative about a third of employees will be in favor, a third will be on the fence, and the remaining third will be opposed. If this arithmetic stays in place, your change program will fail. Charlotte Beers kept this formula in mind when she launched the very successful turnaround of the firm some years back, and later claimed that this mind-set forced her to address the issue of identifying and dealing with resistance. While no statistically proven research supports these exact numbers—and, of course, each situation will be different—Beers's formula is as good a working assumption as any.

The task—indeed, the imperative—is to change the initial arithmetic as quickly as possible. An effective way to counter resistance is to maximize participation in what needs to be done. People support what they help to build. It is particularly important to recruit some of the fence-sitters in the endeavor, and maybe even some of the initial resisters.

For maximum effectiveness, commitment through involvement should begin right at the start of the strategy process, not just at the end of it. A strategy conceived by a small team at the top, deliberating behind closed doors, and then announcing to the organization "Here, do this" will seldom win full-hearted support. Mapping out the future of your organization in secret sends a message of distrust. It also suggests inadequacy on the part of the larger team: "This stuff is too important for you to be involved in. We do the thinking and you act on it." Grudging compliance will be about all you can expect.

That's why the Strategic Learning process is a team-based approach. Create as much participation in the process as possible, with multifunctional teams developing insights through the Situation Analysis and crystallizing the Strategic Choices. Provide wide visibility throughout the organization about what is going on, who is involved, what the timelines are, and how people can contribute their ideas along the way. (The Girl Scouts, for example, set up an interactive website to keep everyone informed and involved.) The result: Not only do you get the benefit of diverse ideas, but you are building commitment as you go along.

Those who want to limit participation in the strategy process sometimes make the argument, "We must preserve confidentiality." I believe that the need for confidentiality is mostly exaggerated. At the end of the day, you will need to share the strategy if you want people to act on it! And what usually happens when you do things in secret is that you cause uncertainty and raise speculation. Everyone knows there are discussions going on, and rumors begin to incite employees' worst fears. What people fear most is uncertainty. Even an unpleasant certainty is usually easier to cope with than uncertainty.

In contrast, research shows that open cultures, which foster the exchange of ideas and the search for truth, are the most adaptive organizations. So the trade-off between confidentiality and transparency will strongly favor transparency, except in the most unusual situations, such as the planning of a surprise move. When that is the case, employees will almost always understand that this exception has been in the common interest.

Commitment versus Consensus

To a lot of people, maximizing participation means achieving consensus. I strongly believe, though, that setting a goal of consensus is a trap that prevents you from achieving the real objective. As one of my client companies says, "Consensus is where we are. Commitment is where we want to be." You have to cultivate participation, but if you take the consensus route, you won't get where you want—and need—to be.

We mustn't confuse commitment with consensus. Commitment is the dedication to a course of action that has been decided on, whether or not one has supported the idea in the preceding discussions. It is built on a shared understanding that is embedded in the organization's culture—a "social contract," if you like. The guiding principle is that breakthrough decisions emerge from an energetic pursuit of the best ideas through vigorous but respectful give-and-take. At a certain point, however, a decision must be made by the leader; and once a decision is made, the understanding is that everyone will close ranks and support the decision with relentless follow-through. The process is divergent, then convergent: learn, *then* focus.

Consensus is something very different. Margaret Thatcher, the former prime minister of Great Britain, summed it up when she said, "Consensus is the process of abandoning all beliefs, principles, and policies in search of something in which no one believes, but to which no one objects; the process of avoiding the very issues that have to be solved."[8] In other words, consensus is a cop-out. It averages down to the lowest common denominator. It may be a noble search for harmony but it produces dilution, a collective pursuit of mediocrity.

Both commitment and consensus produce social cohesion. But there is a big difference in the means of getting there. Commitment organizations are driven by the pursuit of the best ideas. Consensus organizations are motivated by agreement for agreement's sake.

Strategically effective organizations are commitment organizations.

Generate Short-Term Wins

Many change programs are long term in nature. The journey to success can take multiple years. The psychology that can set in is that victory is far away, that it has little to do with daily activities—almost as if ultimate success will arrive on the appointed day, with nothing of much consequence happening in between. When this happens, the momentum behind the change initiative will wane and a wait-and-see attitude will take hold.

One purpose of the gap-closing process (described in Chapter 6) is to ensure that the pathway from the present state to the desired future state is mapped out with clarity, and that accountability for results is clearly defined. That will provide a vivid vision of success and instill project management discipline into the effort.

But there is another, equally important, goal for the gap-closing process: to ensure that there is a sense of energy, progress, and enthusiasm that will propel the organization forward. This is about igniting the human spirit and instilling the belief that what needs to be done *can* be done.

I was recently working with gap teams on a strategy initiative for a company in the healthcare industry. The insights from their Situation Analysis had demonstrated the need for a major shift in strategy based on the fundamental changes going on in the industry. They had developed a crystal-clear Winning Proposition and five Key Priorities. Everyone was convinced and committed to the change.

The gap teams had been diligently working during the prior three months on the present state, future state, obstacles, and milestones for each priority. The quality of the work was excellent, and there was a real sense of confidence that this organization had a good handle on what needed to be done, by whom, by when.

There was only one problem. All the milestones for the critical results were two or three years away. As this realization sank in, a palpable feeling of letdown pervaded the room: "The jury is out for at least two years. We won't know until then whether we have succeeded." While the mood was still very businesslike and filled with expectation, what was missing was *belief*. I could sense this same mental state in the gap team members themselves. The energy was drained by the sense that something was missing.

Then one of the strategy team—let's call him Bill—spoke up. Bill articulated what everyone was thinking with his pointed question: "What have we already achieved in closing these gaps that demonstrates we are winning?" The gap champions eagerly reported their short-term wins, and suddenly expectation sparked into belief. Instead of "wait and see," the mood changed to "we're confident we can." There was a surge of enthusiasm.

Immediately, it was decided that the gap teams would define further short-term outputs for dates one month, three months, six months out, and beyond. These results would give the organization the chance to celebrate its early successes and deal promptly with problem areas. The coordinator of the gap teams summed up the new approach: "We're going from knowing to doing to excelling to *accelerating*."

Everyone left the meeting with an extra spring in their step.

Deal Directly with Resisters

In all major change efforts, you will inevitably encounter a pocket of resisters who oppose the change for a variety of emotional, psychological, and only sometimes rational reasons. Some of these holdouts are outspoken, while others—I call them the silent assassins—quietly and insidiously maneuver to obstruct the changes. The interesting thing about this is that the whole organization knows what is going on and is watching the contest of wills. Leaders who fail to perceive these realities and deal decisively but fairly with the resisters will doom their change initiative.

I recall having to deal with just such a problem when I was the newly appointed president of Seagram USA. Seagram had a wide range of distilled spirits brands, which by law had to be sold through a national system of independent distributors, which in turn sold these products to the retail trade. This was the so-called three-tier system that everyone in the industry had to comply with. These distributors also carried competitive products, so it was vitally important to cultivate the support of the distributors to push your brands. The distributors, of course, were prone to favor the suppliers that provided the biggest profit opportunity for them.

As part of a business review, we assessed the profit contribution for each of Seagram's brands, using the Portfolio Profitability Map described in Chapter 4. This showed clearly that there were 37 brands that were underperforming and dragging down the overall profitability of the business. Just as seriously, devoting scarce resources to making and selling these less-profitable brands was diluting the focus on the premium brands, which represented our best hope for a profitable future. To me, and others in my team, the answer was clear: Sell these 37 brands and concentrate on the premium brands.

Then I ran into a serious source of resistance from a longtime Seagram veteran, and one of my key subordinates. Andrew (not his real name) was highly influential in the organization, an astute political operator, and openly admitted he was disappointed at not getting my job. He typically expressed his views with almost intimidating bluntness. I was the newcomer, hired from the outside, with a background in foods and limited experience in distilled spirits.

Andrew was part of the meeting during which the team had reviewed brand profitability and concluded that streamlining the portfolio was the best way forward. He had made some curt counterarguments then lapsed into a sullen red-faced silence. It was clear he hated the decision.

A few minutes after the meeting ended, Andrew marched into my office and purposefully closed the door. He had a grim look on his face. "Look," he said, "let me put you straight. Selling these brands would be a disaster for this company. The distributors will pay less attention to our portfolio, and the whole business will suffer." Then came the zinger. He said, "Willie, you are making a mistake out of ignorance about how this business works. You're a foods guy, not a liquor guy. It's obvious to me this is a bad decision. The other members of the team are simply 'yessing' you to death."

I had little doubt that Andrew was acting sincerely but mainly out of emotion. He had a sentimental attachment to the brands he had been marketing zealously for over 20 years. He was also fiercely loyal to his people, and was clearly concerned about the inevitable layoffs that would result from the spin-off of the 37 brands. But these were unspoken reasons. His intellectual argument was based on the potential adverse reaction from our distributors, who would have a lower level of overall volume from our reduced (but more profitable) brand portfolio if we eliminated these brands.

My concern was that Andrew might use his political clout to resist the decision, and that if I went ahead against his wishes he might (albeit subconsciously) be inclined to undermine any favorable results.

I decided to focus on the spoken arguments Andrew had raised about negative distributor reaction to a possible sell-off of the 37 brands. After all, this was something we could objectively evaluate. I invited him to join me on a whistle-stop tour to visit our key distributors and get their reactions firsthand. I assured him he would be free to make his side of the argument. Many of the distributors were his personal friends.

The following week, Andrew and I went on our tour. I don't think there were many people in the company who weren't aware of this fact-finding trip, and no doubt speculation about the outcome was pervasive. A side benefit was that the two of us had the chance to chat informally during plane rides, and gradually a personal connection began to develop.

The distributor meetings were a revelation. I had expected them to lean in favor of streamlining, but without exception the distributors strongly supported the sell-off as a winning strategy. In fact, they pleaded with us to do it as quickly as we could. They wanted to clear away the dead wood and focus on the important brands as the most profitable strategy for the long term.

At first, Andrew simply acquiesced. I sensed that he wouldn't interfere with the decision, but I wasn't sure he would support it. This was not good. The business case on its own was compelling, but without his committed support it was not going be as successful as it could be.

I met with Andrew for a candid conversation and laid it on the line. I explained that I understood his concerns about layoffs, but promised that we would handle these with dignity and generosity. I told him that I needed his active support, that nothing else would be good enough. I confirmed my expectations in a written note I had prepared so there could be no misunderstanding. He read the note, paused for a few seconds, and then declared himself. "I assure you of my total support," he said, and we shook hands.

Andrew was true to his word. He became a champion of the plan. We divested the 37 brands, dealt fairly and compassionately with the layoffs, and concentrated our resources on the remaining premium brands. Within four years of this action, Seagram's spirits business, excluding the brands we had spun off, realized a 36 percent increase in profits over what it had generated when it included those brands.

This story has a nice grace note. About a year into the new strategy, Andrew wrote me a letter apologizing for opposing the plan in the first place, and renewing his promise of support. It was a generous thing for a proud man to do. Afterward, I noticed a quickening of his efforts to make the plan work, and saw the sales numbers rise a little faster. Therein lay this counter-intuitive insight: Those who start off as your detractors can often end up being your strongest allies.

The situation had been tricky to deal with. In many ways, I navigated through it on instinct. But the lessons it taught me have guided my approach to resisters ever since:

▼ The whole organization is watching how you deal with this moment of truth.

▼ You must deal firmly but fairly with resisters, or your support from the rest of the organization will melt away.

▼ If you wait too long, resistance will generate a momentum of its own.

▼ The intellectual arguments of resisters will seldom reveal their underlying motivations.

There is another important leadership principle here. To tolerate resisters is to apply a double standard: one set of expectations for those who support the strategy and a different one for those who are allowed to continue opposing what is in the common interest.

In the final analysis, if resisters dig in their heels and remain intransigent, then you have to take decisive action to either move them to a different part of the organization or ask them to leave. You should give them every chance you can before you take that step, but if they continue to undermine the change, either as an overt protestor or as a silent assassin, then you owe it to the organization not to perpetuate a double standard. Don't assume that no one will notice. The organization is watching and waiting for you to take action. Everyone is hoping your persuasion will prevail, and that if it doesn't succeed, you'll remove the source of resistance before it spreads.

Set a Shining Example

The importance of setting an example goes straight to the heart of leadership. Above all, it's what leaders *do*, not just what they *say*, that speaks the loudest about what they believe in. The moment your words and deeds come apart, your leadership is dead. At times of major change, your followers are scrutinizing your every deed and gesture. There is symbolic importance in everything you do. Nothing is neutral.

An inspirational example of this great principle is Nelson Mandela, who led South Africa safely from the appalling apartheid era into a democracy. Most people are familiar with the background to this story. Mandela was imprisoned for 27 years on Robben Island, off the shores of Cape Town, for his opposition to apartheid. He was eventually released and became the first democratically elected president of the country. But the real drama of the story was about to unfold.

When Mandela took office, South Africa held its breath. Anger among black South Africans had reached boiling point. After years of privation, there was massive unemployment and huge deficiencies in healthcare, housing, and education for black people. Mandela was their hero. They expected him to extract retribution from the whites to assuage their anger. There was a groundswell of belief among the blacks that it was payback time. This would have been the popular thing to do.

But Mandela understood that raw violence would be unleashed by any such actions, and that the effects of such violence would be devastating. Mandela made a remarkable speech in which he made clear that he was the leader of South Africans of all races; that he cared for them all equally; that his commitment was to forgive and reconcile; and that his vision was to create a "rainbow nation" of all South Africans living in peace and working together to create a great future. It was a great unifying moment.

Mandela followed his words with actions. The now-famous Truth and Reconciliation Commission was established to allow those who had abused power and administered cruelty and injustice to admit their past offenses and receive forgiveness. Those who refused to do this were given a fair criminal trial, and punished if found guilty. Mandela's every gesture and daily agenda reinforced the theme of unity and reconciliation. He even became a supporter of South Africa's national rugby team, historically comprised almost entirely of white South Africans, and therefore an emblem of white supremacy.

Few realize how close South Africa had come to civil war. Against all the odds, Mandela had led the nation through an unprecedented peaceful revolution and had won the admiration, deep affection, and profound support of all South Africans. This was as close to a miracle as it gets.

A few years ago, Bill Clinton, the former U.S. president visited Mandela in South Africa. Mandela showed him around Robben Island, pointing out where he had spent all those years in prison, and explained the events that followed. Clinton was deeply moved and reportedly asked Mandela if he hadn't felt the need for retribution. Mandela's reply: "No, I didn't. If I had, I would never have left prison. But it would have been a prison of my own making."

The majestic role model that Mandela provided serves as a great lesson to all of us. The key to successful leadership is to embody the change we seek to create. All else follows from there.

8

Translating Your Strategy into a Compelling Leadership Message

People will do almost any what *if you give them a good* why.
— Nietzsche

We come now to the fourth and final golden rule for the effective implementation of your strategy: *Create a simple leadership message to win the hearts and minds of employees, and repeat it continuously* (Figure 8.1).

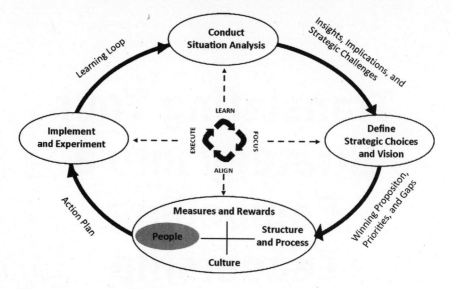

Figure 8.1 Leading through Strategic Learning: Align

Some years ago I was asked to help an organization in the specialty chemicals industry with the implementation of its strategy. The CEO emphasized that the strategy had already been clearly defined and communicated. All that was required was for the organization to act on it. He wanted guidance on best practices in the field of strategy implementation. "This organization is hopeless at execution, and I'm really getting impatient with the lack of urgency around here," he said. "Please help us instill the right disciplines."

As a first step, I asked if I could conduct some interviews to try to diagnose where the problems lay. This was willingly arranged, and in the following weeks I spoke to a wide range of employees at various levels in the company.

The results were startling. Not a single person could give a simple explanation of the company's strategy. More to the point, when I asked if they could offer a compelling reason why customers should choose to do business with their company, most gave vague, rambling answers; a few even looked surprised by the question. Perhaps most important, no one was clear what the key priorities were for the organization or where their department fit into that picture. Needless to say, there was not much excitement around the place.

But there was one thing everyone did remember. Some months previously, there had been a global meeting of all key employees. The event featured golf and all manner of other recreational pursuits, which were very enjoyable. And, of course, there was a series of PowerPoint presentations by the executive team, laying out the plans and expectations for the years ahead. Could they remember what was said? "Oh yes," they said. "We must grow faster and improve our bottom line." That was the closest understanding they had of the strategy for the company.

Soon after, I met with the CEO and his executive team to report my findings. I quickly came to the point. "I don't believe you have an implementation problem," I told them. "In the minds of your employees, you don't actually have a strategy." There was an awkward silence and then the CEO jumped out his chair and strode over to a flipchart at the end of the table. He was very worked up. "Of course, we have a strategy," he said. "Let me show it to you." He proceeded to portray the strategy in simple graphic terms, with a clear statement of the priorities, flipping over the sheets energetically as he sketched it out. It was an impressive performance. "I know this is hard to take," I responded, "but unless the strategy you have so clearly described lives in the hearts and minds of all your employees, you don't really have one."

To the CEO's credit, he accepted the point. Crafting a winning strategy was only the starting point for collective action. The big global meeting, with all those formal presentations, was no substitute for effective leadership communication. The executive team immediately got down to the task of creating a communications campaign in which each member would play a role. The strategy document would be translated into a simple, compelling leadership message and communicated in a series of meetings and workshops. That simple message would serve as the basis for applying the basic implementation disciplines I have been discussing in this book.

My point is this: For a strategy to be supported and acted upon, it has to live in the hearts and minds of employees. We must get rid of the notion that the final product of a strategy is a document. The documentation of a strategy is a vital discipline, but it is the *platform* for strategic leadership, not the end point. Moreover, a sterile

PowerPoint presentation of that document is unlikely to move an organization to action. We need to think of a strategy as a leadership story.

What Is Leadership?

Effective communication is one of the core tasks of a leader. With that in mind, Howard Gardner in *Five Minds for the Future* offers the best definition of leadership that I have come across: "A leader is someone who is able, through persuasion and personal example, to change the *thoughts*, *feelings*, and *behaviors* of those whom he seeks to lead."[1]

Gardner's description of leadership is useful because it identifies the crucial elements that must work together for leaders to be effective. To begin with, it reminds us that leaders move people to action both through their words and the example they set. Furthermore, effective leaders don't just seek to change the behavior of others; that gets you nothing more than compliance.

It is the combination of thoughts, feelings, and behaviors that produces commitment. And the difference between compliance and commitment is the bridge between doing and excelling.

Let's take a moment to examine the three crucial elements more fully:

> *How people think.* This involves leadership as teaching. If we expect our employees to think and function strategically, we need to take the time to give them a clear understanding of important matters, such as the aims of the organization, the nature of the competitive environment, the needs of customers, and the drivers of the firm's economic engine. We must influence the mind-set they apply to their daily challenges and decisions.
>
> *How people feel.* Leaders are the chief motivation officers of their teams. What they do and say must build trust, commitment, and enthusiasm. Employees have a limited amount of emotional and creative energy to devote to the various aspects of their lives. They need good reasons to bring more of themselves to their work.

How people behave. To achieve concerted action, the efforts and energies of everyone should be aligned behind the Winning Proposition and Key Priorities of the organization, in a process of translation from the top level to all the levels below. In addition, it is vital, as explained in Chapter 6, that there is collective adherence to the cultural norms and behaviors of the organization, as the glue that keeps everyone working together.

Building a Cathedral

The following short morality tale illustrates these key principles of leadership. A man walking along the sidewalk comes across three workers toiling away at a construction site. He stops, and asks the first worker, "What are you doing?" The worker answers, "I'm digging a hole." He poses the same question to the second worker, who replies, "I'm laying bricks." Finally, he turns to the third worker, "And what are you doing?" The third worker answers, "I'm building a cathedral."

The essential task of a leader is to be able to describe "the cathedral"—the cause worth working for. This gives meaning to everyone's role, no matter how humble. It enables the leader to say to the first worker, "You're not just digging a hole. You are helping to create strong foundations for this cathedral, so it will stand for a thousand years." And to the second worker, "You are not just laying bricks. You are helping to create a beautiful façade for this cathedral, so it will be admired by all who see it."

Leaders should—and can—always evoke a mental picture of the cathedral that will inspire their people and give meaning to mundane tasks. One manager at a company that manufactures, among other things, satellite components tells his teams, "You're not just soldering motherboards. You're an integral part of our national defense system." To prove that his words aren't just hot air, he regularly brings aerospace and military personnel for tours of the manufacturing facilities, and these people, too, reinforce the message that even the smallest task has significance.

Parents attempting to teach their children courtesy often say, "People will forget what you did. They will forget what you said. But they won't forget the way you made them feel." The same lesson holds true for leaders: Make your people feel that their efforts are valued—and valuable—and they will trust and support your strategy.

Commander's Intent

The Army War College in Carlisle, Pennsylvania, is a postgraduate education center for military leaders, often referred to as the "school for generals." I have run a number of seminars there that bring together organizational leaders from the military, commercial, and not-for-profit sectors, as well as faculty members from both Columbia Business School and the Army War College. We don't go there to learn how to make war. Our aim is to explore the big issues of strategy and leadership and to learn from each other. These seminars invariably produce rich insights as the participants look at these issues with fresh eyes.

Part of the curriculum is a guided tour of the Gettysburg battlefield and an exploration of the various challenges of choice-making, motivation, and leadership that arose in that historic Civil War battle. Some of the universal lessons of leadership emerge more starkly from military theory and practice, simply because war is a matter of life and death. This concentrates the mind on what is important and what isn't.

The military concept of "commander's intent" always strikes a chord with civilian leaders.[2] In the past, military commanders were taught to issue clear battle orders, so that troops in the field knew exactly what was expected of them. Ambiguity on the field of battle can have fatal consequences, so great emphasis was placed on issuing these orders in very specific, unequivocal terms. An example might be ordering troops to capture a particular bridge in a specific location, say three days' march away. Now, it could happen that the strike force would march the three days to the bridge, only to find the bridge so heavily fortified that it is impossible to capture. After all this effort and time, this result would be reported back to the commanding officer. The bridge clearly could not be taken. At this point, the commander might explain that the purpose of capturing the bridge had been to cut off the supply lines of the enemy. "If we had known that at the time," the strike force leader might have said, "we could have found a way across the river and cut off the road further up the supply line."

Today, aspiring generals at the Army War College are taught not only to define battle orders but to frame a commander's intent. This involves clearly explaining the *ultimate purpose* of the actions you are asking your troops to take. It's not enough to say "capture that bridge." Commander's intent requires that you explain the ultimate purpose—"to cut off the supply lines of the enemy"—with taking the bridge as one possible method of accomplishing this.

Commander's intent accomplishes two important leadership goals. The first: It is a basic fact of human nature that people will fight harder for a cause they believe is worthy of their effort and sacrifice. As Nietzsche said, they will do almost any what if you give them a good why. The second goal is about flexibility and empowerment. Battlefields are chaotic. They are filled with unexpected developments, obstacles, and opportunities. Field forces that understand the ultimate purpose of their engagement with the enemy are able to react to these emergent factors with better strategic decisions and faster actions in the heat of battle.

The concept of commander's intent is a profoundly important principle in the leadership of organizations, and speaks directly to Strategic Learning's insight-to-action approach to decision-making. While, thankfully, few decisions in the commercial and not-for-profit sectors are a matter of human life and death, as they can be in the military, they nevertheless go to the core of an organization's ability to survive and thrive. To be effective, leaders must be able to describe not just the goal but the intention behind the goal and how everyone's role fits into that larger cause.

Who Are the Leaders?

Whose job is it to translate your organization's strategy from a document into a compelling leadership message that will win the hearts and minds of employees? It is everyone's job at every level in the organization.

It is easy to lapse into the comfortable notion that it is the exclusive responsibility of the head of the organization. Then we can simply sit back and ask, "Why don't our leaders do this?" But this is not the way strategically coherent organizations work.

Let me emphasize a crucial point I made earlier in this book. For an organization to win, leaders at every level must develop a clear line of sight to the organization's overall Winning Proposition and Key Priorities and then translate these into an aligned Winning Proposition and Key Priorities for their domains of responsibility. Everything that happens at every level in an organization should support the overall priorities of the enterprise. These are the only actions that create value. Everything else just adds costs. Nothing is neutral.

Developing a clear line of sight to the organization's overall strategic goals is not straightforward. Clarity will not descend as a gift out of the blue. The prerequisite is for every leader to take personal responsibility for making it happen. It is an inherent obligation of a leader to establish the necessary degree of clarity and simplicity, to describe the "cathedral" that gives meaning to the work of employees. It is no excuse to plead that the top leadership has not made it clear enough. As Shakespeare wrote in *Julius Caesar*, "The fault, dear Brutus, lies not in our stars, but in ourselves."[3]

For example, when the various local councils within the Girl Scouts create their individual strategies, the essential starting point is the line of sight to the mission for the overall movement: to be the premier leadership experience for girls. From there, the councils translate the mission into local strategies, taking account of local market circumstances, local competitors, and the specific needs of their local customers. Each council then devises a clear Winning Proposition and set of Key Priorities that both satisfy its local market and align with the national strategy.

As the Girl Scouts expands among immigrant communities, local councils have had to adapt to ensure their programs are within the context of the newcomers' experience, culture, and faith. Latino families often need to be reassured that camping doesn't mean sending their daughters into the forest all alone. Muslim cultures need to know that their girls won't be expected to swim in immodest attire. Some troops speak only Spanish, or Vietnamese, or Urdu, and some speak a mixture of English and their mother tongue. The common denominator, though, is the overall Girl Scouts mission: Teaching girls to become leaders in their own lives. That's a goal that transcends all cultural boundaries.

The Questions on the Minds of Employees

George Bernard Shaw once remarked, "The problem with communication is the illusion that it has occurred."[4] We hold fondly to the belief that once we have articulated what we want to say, then everyone has understood it, is convinced by it, and will act on it. But winning hearts and minds is a more demanding job than that.

An essential quality of good communication is being a good listener. This means understanding what is going on in the minds of employees. The ultimate art of good listening is to hear what is *not* being said, but what is nevertheless being felt. This was once described to me as "hearing the music between the words." As leaders tackle the task of communicating the organization's strategy, the following questions are almost always on the minds of employees, and if they are not answered clearly and credibly, employees will simply tune out.

▼ What are we aiming to achieve, and why should I care?

▼ Where does my department fit in, and what is expected of me?

▼ How will we measure success, and what's in it for me?

In communicating the organization's strategy, each of these issues must be specifically addressed. Motivation happens at the individual level. Employees cannot be expected to excel unless they know what is expected of them and why.

Developing Your Leadership Message

The real question is not just how to communicate effectively in a general sense. It is how to communicate your *strategy* so that it wins the hearts and minds of your employees. It has been said that the best leaders, almost without exception and at every level, are master users of stories and symbols. Think of Jesus's use of parables, Churchill's resonating phrases, even Steve Jobs's ability to describe, as he puts it, an "insanely great" lifestyle that's attainable with the purchase of just a few key gadgets.

We have talked in detail about the four steps of the Strategic Learning process: Learn, Focus, Align, and Execute. Giving these steps the attention and commitment they deserve will ensure that all the key elements of a winning strategy have been clearly defined. But what does it take to communicate those elements in an utterly simple way so that you are able to change the thoughts, feelings, and behaviors of employees?

All effective communication of a strategy, including the answers to the key questions on the minds of employees, can be boiled down into four headings: Why, What, How, How Much.

> *The Why.* This consists of a concise summary of the brutal truths from the Situation Analysis. These insights provide the essential "reason why" for the Strategic Choices. This summary should always put the customer hierarchy of needs at center stage. Without a good why, the what will be meaningless.
>
> *The What.* This provides a simple explanation of the Strategic Choices, answering these questions:
>
> ▼ Where will we compete?
>
> ▼ What will we offer our chosen customers?
>
> ▼ What is our Winning Proposition?
>
> ▼ What are our Key Priorities?
>
> The what and the why should hang together in a seamless flow of logic.
>
> *The How.* This describes how the strategy will be implemented and what is expected of everyone at every level. It covers:
>
> ▼ The gap statements and the role of the gap teams
>
> ▼ How all the elements of the business system will be aligned behind the strategy
>
> ▼ A clear explanation of roles and responsibilities

The How Much. This provides a convincing statement of the economic logic of the strategy and lays out the financial and operational targets being aimed at. In other words, it clarifies "the size of the prize."

It's not just a question of putting content underneath each of these headings. Effective leaders are able to weave these elements together into an integrated and engaging story. Even the most brilliant strategies will not energize employees unless leaders are able to do this.

Note that I keep emphasizing that your leadership message must be "compelling." This means developing the skills of good storytelling. It is well established that people learn best through stories. We tend to dismiss this as the way children learn. But it actually applies equally well to adults.

Great stories share some common features. They are simple, not complicated. They capture the imagination through vivid examples, metaphors, and pictures. They involve human beings, not just dry information. They follow a clear story line. The call to action is clearly framed. Last but not least, they are genuine—the storyteller embodies the message. After all, have you ever come across a great leader who is not able to simplify complexity through examples and stories?

Some leaders are "naturals" at storytelling. For others, it is a skill to be learned. Whatever your starting point, it is a skill you can develop through the disciplines of deliberate practice.

The Power of Storytelling

There is a popular myth that if you can run a business, then it's automatic that you can also teach. Having run businesses over a period of 20 years, I readily fell prey to this assumption when I started teaching at Columbia Business School some 14 years ago. I quickly bumped into harsh reality. Teaching is a different skill, one you have to learn over time. And the learning process is never-ending. You are always stretching to the next level of excellence. That's what makes it so challenging and so rewarding.

We learn best when the feedback loops from our actions are immediate and truthful. In teaching, the feedback loops are instantaneous and unforgiving. You can sense in real time when participants are not engaged. Energy sags. Eyes glaze. The BlackBerries surreptitiously emerge. There's no learning going on.

You can also tell right away when those magic "aha" moments occur. Participants sit forward in their chairs. They scribble notes. They raise their hands to get into a discussion, and dig down deeper. The energy level rises palpably. Learning is happening.

When do those magic moments of learning occur? Almost invariably in my seminars they happen when I use an example, picture, or metaphor to illustrate my point; hardly ever when I rely on reason by itself. At the end of a one-week program, participants go through an exercise to summarize their most valuable insights—those they believe will help them excel back in the workplace. What is striking is how often they will point to a story or example I used during the week and the meaning they have extracted from these.

Paradoxically, metaphors are effective precisely because they are seldom complete in themselves. Listeners must use their imagination to complete the picture, and as co-creators they will feel a greater sense of ownership of the underlying insight. Storytelling is powerful because it invites this process of co-creation.

Here's a mental experiment. Throughout this book I have endeavored to use stories and metaphors to help clarify concepts. Think for a moment about the ideas that have (I hope) been most memorable. I will wager that among these have been:

▼ The value/cost elastic band (Mind the gap!)

▼ The parable of the gearbox

▼ The 80/20 rule

▼ The arithmetic of business

▼ The geranium story

▼ The General Motors saga

▼ The lessons of the sigmoid curve

If any of these are the ones you remember, I suggest it's because they conveyed a key idea with a simple mental picture.

One of the points I have been emphasizing is the need to have a genuine Winning Proposition, not a mere Value Proposition. This important concept is based on the reality that in a competitive environment, absolutes have no meaning. Everything is comparative. Thus, we have to give our customers a compelling reason to choose our offerings over the competing alternatives. This margin of difference in the value we deliver is what competitive advantage is all about.

Now let me make the identical point with a story I heard at a management conference a few years back. I can't vouch for its accuracy, but I found the story an engaging way of illustrating this very same concept. Here it is:

> ALPO dog food is a leading brand in the U.S. pet food market. At a certain point, ALPO was losing market share. The management tried various things to turn around the fortunes of the brand, but nothing seemed to work. The CEO became exasperated and called a meeting of the key executives. He threw down the gauntlet with a series of provocative questions. "We have the most nutritionally advanced product in the industry, right?" "Yes," came back the reply. "We have most attractive packaging, right?" Again, a chorus of yesses. "And ALPO has the best advertising, retail distribution, and shelf displays, right?" "Yes, it does." "So, then," thundered the CEO, "why is our market share going down?" A voice from the back called out, "Because the dogs don't like it!"

Now, do you have a more memorable way to think about the importance of a Winning Proposition?

The Need for Repetition

A leadership message is not a one-time event. It's a campaign. The key is to reinforce the message as often as possible, in both formal and informal settings. In informal settings, it is particularly effective to "connect the dots" by showing how everyday activities and challenges tie back to the Winning Proposition and Key Priorities. As Dr. Ash Tewari emphasized, "Always keep the main thing the main thing."

It helps to have other members of your team telling the same story in their own words. Try to keep the story fresh by keeping the examples up to date. The golden rule is to simplify complexity.

One additional reason for repetition is management turnover. In any 12-month period, for example, there is likely to be a number of new members in the rank and file, people who have never heard the leadership message.

Of course, in times of crisis or significant change, effective leadership communication counts more than ever. The key is to be a truth-teller; no sugarcoating. When people are left in the dark, they invent their own realities. This is how rumors begin, and once they get underway, they are hard to counteract.

A compelling leadership message is not so much a matter of eloquence, although that can help. The qualities that resonate most strongly are honesty, authenticity, simplicity, and humanity. More important than silver-tongued oratory is to be a straight shooter.

One of the best examplars I know of this kind of leadership communication is Kathy Cloninger, the CEO of the Girl Scouts of the USA. As I mentioned earlier, the Girl Scouts has undertaken a major transformation, filled with numerous challenges and obstacles. Kathy has repeated her message of change over and over again to audiences throughout the organization. Kathy embodies her message. She is unwavering in her belief that success will be achieved, while being realistic about the barriers that must be overcome. Her message is always simple and readily understandable to everyone. It is tuned exactly to the questions and concerns in the minds of employees. As always happens, there is a human toll involved in this kind of transformation. Kathy's intense empathy, compassion, and respect for human dignity have bolstered the morale of employees during this journey of change.

Through your leadership message, you are not just explaining your organization's strategy. You are expressing who you are and what you stand for as a leader.

Execute

Implementing and Experimenting in the Strategic Learning Cycle

One must learn by doing the thing, for though you think you know it, you have no certainty unless you try.

—Aristotle

How many times have you heard the following claim: "The hard part of a strategy is getting it done; the rest is easy."? No one will disagree that it's actions that make the cash register ring. Effective implementation is vitally important. But just beating a drum about implementation misses the larger point: Strategy creation and strategy implementation are mutually interdependent. The one cannot work without the other.

Implementation, like the bottom line, is not a thing apart. After all, the *entire* Strategic Learning process—Learn, Focus, Align, and Execute—is a challenge of implementation. Each stage of the process has its own set of hurdles and rewards, and when done effectively, each stage builds on the previous one to generate a powerful

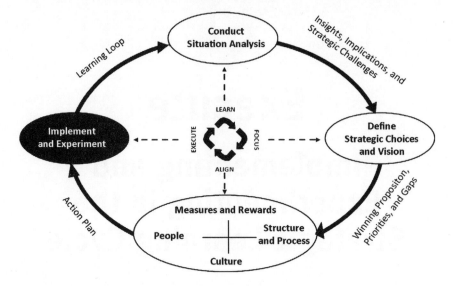

Figure 9.1 Leading through Strategic Learning: Execute

momentum behind your strategy. Every step helps to bridge the gap between doing and excelling.

If all of the components of the Strategic Learning process are in place, then this cohesion will help you to execute your plan rapidly and successfully. But the implementation of your strategy will only be as effective as your insight, focus, and alignment, and the quality of those outputs will depend on the rigor of your discipline as you go through each of these steps. If an organization constructs its strategy in a piecemeal fashion, fails to build it on solid insights, or neglects to consider how it will align the levers of its business system behind its strategy, then its chances of success are slender.

That's why implementation should be seen as part of the continuum of the Strategic Learning cycle (Figure 9.1). It represents both its successful culmination and a source of learning for the continuation of the cycle.

Learning through Experimentation

Great execution is not just about doing. It is also about learning from what you do, so you keep doing it better. The gap between doing and excelling is a learning gap. Strategic Learning is essentially an insight-to-action-to-insight cycle. It is about learning your way to excellence.

One of the most crucial activities involved in the Execute stage of the cycle is experimentation. Experimentation injects a different kind of divergent learning. The Situation Analysis is an intellectual voyage of discovery. Experimentation adds to this the dimension of learning through action.

We can't figure out everything that will and won't work through pure analysis or market research. A hypothesis is a good starting point, but then we often need a proving ground of some kind—for example, to determine the optimal price point, customers' response to different product features or what it takes to succeed in a new market.

Strategic choices are all about risk and probability. Just because you make a strategic choice doesn't mean you can't say, "This is the strategy we're going to follow. We had to make a choice and we made it according to our best judgment. However, one of the alternative choices also looked promising. So while we're going to go full steam ahead on implementing our chosen strategy, we'll explore that other possibility through a controlled experiment in a small area, see what we learn, and then scale up those lessons."

For example, as I wrote this book, consumer products giant Procter & Gamble was taking a hit on Tide, its top-selling brand in the United States. Cash-strapped consumers were switching to cheaper brands, even if they lacked some of Tide's cleaning capabilities.[1] The big issue P&G faced was this: "With so many consumers buying less-expensive, private-label brands, it is obvious that there is lots of business to be had at the lower-cost end of the price spectrum. If we introduce a cheaper version of Tide, will it pull volume from the competing brands or will it cannibalize the mother brand?" Analysis alone can seldom find a good answer to a question like this. The right thing to do is conduct an experiment. And that's exactly what P&G did in testing Tide Basic, a lower-priced version, in 100 stores throughout the South.

A readiness to experiment, to learn from the results, and to adjust your strategy accordingly is a hallmark of adaptive organizations. It mitigates the tendency for thinking to become narrowed within a set of fixed mental models, and it helps stamp out the complacent "If it ain't broke, don't fix it" attitude I've warned against.

As we have seen, rigidity can be fatal when the environment shifts. Charles Darwin showed that the success with which life on earth has evolved to fill almost every conceivable niche in widely varying environments is based on nature's continual experimentation—the generation of an endless stream of variations through the random mechanism of the genetic lottery. In effect, nature places millions of unpremeditated bets on a proliferating array of new variations. Most fail and die out. Those that survive multiply and eventually dominate. Any species that stops adapting is doomed.

The adaptive organization employs a similar methodology. By continually experimenting, producing "mutant strains" of new products, processes, methods, and strategies, the organization maximizes its chances of developing favorable variations that are capable of responding to the next change in the environment.

But as I noted in Chapter 3, this method is different in a crucial way from nature's blind process. Being human, and therefore capable of reason, analysis, insight, and memory, the leaders in an adaptive organization can *learn* from both their mistakes and their successes, and thereby improve their odds of success.

Learning from Others

As the twin forces of globalization and the Internet have made the world smaller and sharpened competition, it is self-limiting to confine yourself to your own experiments. Learn also from other people's experiments.

That's what P&G did when it realized that its famous research and development operation was no longer up to the task of supplying enough ideas for the future. Historically, the company had been very reliant on internally driven innovation. But by 2000, wrote Larry Huston, then P&G's vice president for innovation and knowledge, and his colleague, Nabil Sakkab, senior vice president for research and development, in an article in *Harvard Business Review* (March,

2006), "It was clear to us that our invent-it-ourselves model was not capable of sustaining high levels of top-line growth."[4]

They came up with a revolutionary idea: create an open innovation system by harnessing talent and ideas from outside the company. The basic premise: What if P&G took its 7,500 R&D people and added to that the 1.6 million R&D people outside of the company in its areas of interest? That would create a talent pool of 1,607,500 R&D people at P&G's disposal. Huston wrote, "We knew that external connections could produce highly profitable innovations. Betting on these connections was the key to future growth."

Within five years, the resulting Connect + Develop model had furnished innovations from the outside to more than 35 percent of P&G's new products being sold in the marketplace, up from 15 percent in 2000. And some 45 percent of the initiatives in the product development pipeline had key elements that were discovered externally. P&G estimates that its R&D productivity has increased by nearly 60 percent. As Huston wrote, "The model works."

Learning from Mistakes

Experimentation can't proceed without mistakes. The problem is, successful organizations are, by definition, organizations that do things right. They are filled with people who are justly proud of their technical, administrative, and managerial prowess, and who have risen within the organization largely because of their ability to make things work—usually the first time. Such people set and meet high personal standards of success; they consider failure a mark of shame and do everything possible to avoid it.

All of this is natural, and even admirable. Yet multiplied across the breadth of an entire company, these human qualities can produce an organization that is risk-averse, shunning uncertainty and error in favor of repeating only what has worked in the past. The measurement and reward systems used by many companies encourage the same tendency. In an organization where punishment, disapproval, career stagnation, or even discharge are the likely response to mistakes, people quickly learn to avoid mistakes when they can and cover them up where they can't. Of course, concealing a failure ensures that no one will learn from it.

Learning from experimentation requires a culture that is both open to risk-taking and capable of learning from mistakes. Risk-taking and mistake-making are, after all, opposite sides of the same coin. The key is to make smart mistakes, rather than stupid ones. Smart mistakes are those where the value of the learning is bigger than the cost of the mistake. This is crucially dependent on an organization's ability to analyze and distill the lessons from its experiments and rapidly share and apply them.

Smart mistakes are a hallmark of cultures that are open and adaptive, like the high-performance cultures described in Chapter 6 that are characterized by collaboration, teamwork, and rapid responsiveness to the needs of customers. Rather than waiting to react to changes in the competitive environment, these organizations aren't afraid to experiment and learn from the results of those experiments so that they can respond swiftly and successfully. Like firefighters who train to deal with a variety of different emergencies, organizations that have "trained" through experimentation will be better able to manage volatility, uncertainty, complexity, and ambiguity, and lay the foundations for long-term success.

One organization that has built experimentation into its DNA is Ideo, the award-winning design firm. "Fail early and often to succeed sooner," is its motto. As Tim Brown, Ideo's CEO, writes in his recent book, *Change by Design*, "Leaders should encourage experimentation and accept that there is nothing wrong with failure as long as it happens early and becomes a source of learning. A vibrant . . . culture will encourage prototyping—quick, cheap, and dirty— as part of the creative process and not just as a way of validating finished ideas."[5]

Experiential Learning: The After-Action Review

Learning from experiments has three basic components: conducting the experiment, studying the success or failure of the experiment, and transferring the lessons learned throughout the organization.

To methodically pursue all three steps requires a great deal of discipline. Many companies are stuck in the plan/act mode and devote little time to reflection, analysis, and self-education. But when the learning is done right, it adds immeasurably to an organization's effectiveness.

One of the most powerful techniques for harnessing the power of experiential learning comes from the United States Army.[6] The idea of learning from experience presents a peculiar dilemma for the leadership of the Army. After all, the ultimate form of competition for which the Army was created and which provides the true test of the Army's methods and strategies is an event that no one wants to experience—namely, a war. But in the new global environment, produced by the end of the Cold War and the emergence of new kinds of international threats and challenges, the American military needed ways to test new weapons and tactics without waiting for a war to erupt.

In response to this challenge, the U.S. Army developed several new tools for generating and disseminating knowledge. At the National Training Center in the Mojave Desert, the Army began fighting virtual wars, large-scale combat exercises pitting one high-tech battle unit against another, with every soldier, tank, helicopter, and plane tracked by satellite and computer. The contests are extreme, and sometimes chaotic, hewing as closely to reality as possible without incurring casualties. The data generated by these simulated wars are then fed into the computer at the Army's Center for Army Lessons Learned (CALL), where they are synthesized and then shared throughout the Army's ranks worldwide.

In this process of action learning, the after-action review (AAR) is a key component. An AAR is usually conducted immediately after a military engagement (simulated or real) in order to drive out lessons learned as the basis for continuous improvement. In the course of an AAR, the participants' subjective interpretation of events and the computers' objective data are compared, producing insights that are often eye-opening.

An AAR typically focuses on four questions:

▼ *What was the intent?* What was the intended strategy at the time the action started? What role was supposed to be played by each unit? What was the desired outcome and how was it supposed to be achieved?

▼ *What actually happened?* In Army parlance, what was the "ground truth," the actual events as they played out in the heat of battle, with all the misunderstanding, disruption, and confusion that inevitably occur when two armies clash?

▼ *Why did it happen?* This is the root-cause analysis. How did the commanders' intent, the adversaries' actions, changes in the environment, and the decisions of individuals combine to produce a specific set of outcomes?

▼ *How can we do better?* What lessons can be learned from the events of this action that will enable Army units in similar future actions to carry out their missions in such a way as to more closely achieve the commanders' intent?

An AAR isn't an open-ended feedback session. Rather, it's a highly structured process designed to ferret out the crucial insights to be gleaned from the battlefield experiment. It normally includes commanders from at least three leadership levels within a given unit, as well as their counterparts from other units who were involved in the action. The AAR dialogue is facilitated by an experienced officer who is trained to help the participants sort out their various and often conflicting viewpoints, arrive at the ground truth, and drive out the learning.

The Army's AAR manual recommends that the time spent on the AAR be divided this way: one quarter to reviewing the ground truth, one quarter to discussing why it happened, and fully half to discussing how to improve. It is crucial to conduct the meeting with honesty, frankness, and mutual respect among all the participants, and it is just as important to learn from successes as from failures. That's why the Army follows five simple guidelines in conducting AARs: no sugarcoating; discover the ground truth; no thin skins; take notes; and call it like you see it.

The AAR is a powerful tool for generating organizational learning from experiments and actual experiences. Every action that you take in implementing your strategy is also an opportunity to learn.

By that definition, everything you do is actually an experiment, even if you don't call it that. No wonder the AAR is now being used at world-class organizations such as British Petroleum (BP), Bechtel, and GE, among others. Consider holding an AAR in the aftermath of any key event, such as:

▼ A major new-product launch or market test

▼ The opening of a new manufacturing facility, retail outlet, or website

▼ A corporate reorganization, merger, or spin-off

▼ An external or internal crisis or turning point, such as an unexpected public relations challenge

In short, any significant event that has the potential to produce valuable learning could be a suitable occasion for the AAR exercise.

Strategic Learning 365 Days a Year

To enjoy the full benefits of Strategic Learning, don't let the process slip into dormancy between planning sessions. The lessons learned from experimentation and implementation feed directly back into the Situation Analysis. The organization updates its insights by examining its own actions and by rescanning the environment, and then modifies its strategies accordingly. As you go through the learning loop and repeat the Strategic Learning cycle, the discipline of the AAR is a powerful tool to help you examine what you have learned from your actions so far.

The process of discovery and renewal should never stop. Instead, take deliberate steps to make the Strategic Learning method an active part of your business culture, so that the cycle of Learn, Focus, Align, and Execute is constantly at work, helping your organization adapt to the ever-changing world in which it operates.

Integrating Strategy and Leadership

Leading through a Crisis

Strategic resilience is not about responding to a onetime crisis. . . . It's about continually anticipating and adjusting to deep trends that can impair the earning power of a business.

—Gary Hamel

B ad things can happen to good companies. No matter how good we may become at sensing and analyzing trends, we cannot foresee everything.

Crises represent our ultimate testing ground. Whether it's the recent financial meltdown and its devastating effects, a massive product recall, a natural catastrophe, or an industrywide slump, a crisis is a leadership tipping point, when specific reactions and decisions determine whether an organization will succeed or fail.

What factors decide which organizations are destroyed or crippled by an unexpected crisis, and which emerge stronger than before? What separates the winners from the losers?

The key to enduring success is not about attempting to jump-start leadership when you are already *in* a crisis by trying to summon up capabilities that didn't exist before. It is the ability to lead *through* a crisis, by drawing on the capabilities and reserves of strength already in place.

It is the central premise of Strategic Learning that the overarching mission of leaders is to create adaptive organizations capable of ongoing learning and renewal as the environment changes. The Strategic Learning process aims to embed the required sense-and-respond capability through its iterative cycle of insight, focus, alignment, execution, and the learning loop back to insight. Above all, Strategic Learning aims to promote resilience.

Dealing Successfully with the Unexpected

I found myself in the heart of the storm of the recent financial crisis while working with the Federal Home Loan Bank (FHLB) of Atlanta, which had asked me to help it apply the Strategic Learning process to update its strategy. FHLBs are government-sponsored enterprises (GSEs) whose role is to provide stable, low-cost funding to their member banks for home mortgages and economic development lending. The FHLBs provide loans only to other banks, not to individuals. With their member banks, they represent the largest collective source of home mortgage and community credit in the United States. They are thus a crucial cog in the liquidity wheel.

When I first started working with the FHLB of Atlanta in June 2008, the financial markets were tightening markedly, but the full-blown crisis had not yet hit. In doing the Situation Analysis, not one of the teams predicted that the credit markets, on which they were dependent for their own source of funds, would suddenly and completely freeze up. Credit tightening, higher costs of borrowing, thinner spreads—all these were scenarios they had carefully analyzed and prudently prepared themselves for. But the total collapse of liquidity was not one of the possibilities that was on their radar screen or that of their regulators at that time. It was, literally, unimaginable.

The FHLB strategy team did an excellent job of analyzing the key trends in the external environment, the needs of their customers, and the bank's own realities. Based on their Situation Analysis, a clear Winning Proposition and Key Priorities were defined, and they embarked on the alignment and implementation steps laid out in the Strategic Learning process. Everything seemed to be well set.

A few months later I received a call from Jill Spencer, the chief strategy officer. The liquidity crisis had hit the bank like a hammer blow. It was now facing a huge impediment in providing credit to its members, the service that lies at the heart of its mission as a GSE. Would I come to Atlanta to facilitate a reassessment of their strategy?

What I found when I got to Atlanta was a team that was understandably shocked, but at the same time focused and deliberate. They were being challenged by a set of circumstances they had never seen before. It was clear that urgent action was required, but they recognized that their response needed to be purposeful and strategic, not arbitrary or impulsive.

There is often a surge of feeling in a crisis, a kind of panic reaction that *everything* needs to change—immediately. This is seldom, if ever, necessary. While some things will need to change, and quickly, other things will need to stay the same, and may actually need to be reinforced.

The FHLB team understood that they needed to distinguish clearly between these two things. It was decided that the best way to do this was to go back to the Situation Analysis that had been done a short time before and use it as the baseline for updating their thinking. The teams reexamined the key insights from this prior work and asked themselves these questions:

▼ Which insights from our Situation Analysis are still valid and which have changed?

▼ What are the most important implications of the new developments for continuing to discharge the bank's mission through this crisis?

▼ In what ways will our Key Priorities need to change in the immediate and longer terms?

The reliance on an already-established method for sense-making in the midst of a crisis helped the team to quickly assess the situation and find a clear way forward.

The key insight was that the causes of the credit freeze were systemic and would need to be addressed at the national policy level. As a GSE with a crucial role in the system, the team concluded that its first duty was to work with the regulatory authorities to provide immediate relief for its member banks and help devise a better set of safeguards for the future. These became the new short-term priorities. The team also concluded that once these hurdles were overcome, the original longer-term priorities were still valid and represented the right direction for the future. The result was that the bank was able to regain its footing and navigate successfully through the crisis.

As the FHLB of Atlanta discovered, the world is messy, and although organizations can and must develop a strong capability to pick up early signals and interpret emerging trends, some things are not predictable. But they also realized that they had the advantage of a discipline that they could use to point them in the right direction.

Learning Your Way Out of a Crisis

Crises by their nature are confusing and destabilizing. When we're engulfed by one, there's a temptation to grasp at anything that we think will restore equilibrium. There's also the very human tendency to misjudge the severity of the crisis. Just as there are those who underestimate it, who try to calm things down by saying, "Oh, no, it's not as bad as we think," there are also those who overestimate it, whose mantra is "The sky is falling, the sky is falling." Because of the clear need for action, crises bring out a stream of subjective assessments, knee-jerk reactions, confusion, misinformation, rumor, and wild speculation. Even in the most stable times, everyone has their own theory of reality; in a crisis, all those innate biases become exaggerated.

But even though the acute state of urgency requires prompt action, it's important to make decisions mindfully and strategically, because those decisions are crucial to an organization's survival. That's why the first order of business is to get a grip on reality, no matter how elusive that seems.

Only when an organization addresses the realities it is facing can it come up with a set of priorities and an action plan to deal with the issue. We may not be able to take control of an external shock, but we can take control of our response to it. Essentially, we can *learn* our way out of a crisis.

In coping effectively with unpredictable events, it helps enormously to have a core process to call upon, a structured way of thinking. FHLB of Atlanta had the Strategic Learning method in place as an organizational capability. But even if your organization hasn't gone through the Strategic Learning process, you can apply its fundamental principles. I call this stripped-down version "speed learning." The simple step-by-step process is presented in Figure 10.1.

---

❶ **Define the problem.**
  • What is the essence of the problem facing us?
  • What are its dimensions?
  • What are its root causes and likely future consequences?
  • Is the change cyclical or structural (or both)?

❷ **Examine the external environment.**
  How will this situation affect:
  • The needs and behaviors of our customers?
  • The likely actions of our competitors?
  • The key trends in our industry?

❸ **Examine your own realities.**
  How will this situation affect:
  • Our sales, profits, and cash flow?
  • The attitude and morale of our people?
  What is the worst – and best-case scenario?

❹ **Define your action plan.**
  • What immediate actions must be taken and by whom?
  • What will be our Key Priorities?
  • How will we measure progress?
  • How will we communicate our plans to our people and our external stakeholders?

Figure 10.1   Speed Learning

Companies in crisis often think, "We'd love to do a strategy, but we just don't have the time right now." "Maybe you don't have the time *not* to do it," is what I would reply. Paradoxically, structured thinking actually helps you to move faster. In a crisis, speed learning provides a road map for moving rapidly from insight to action.

The late U.S. senator from New York, Daniel Patrick Moynihan, once said, "You are entitled to your own opinion, but you are not entitled to your own facts."[1] To stabilize the organization, it is essential that the entire leadership team confronts the same reality. There is no stronger accelerator of collective effort than a plain definition of the problem to be solved, together with a clear set of priorities that everyone is acting on.

Building Readiness

While there are steps organizations can take to regain their equilibrium in a crisis, their ability to deal with the unexpected comes mainly from foundations they have already laid. The ultimate protection is to build resilience into your organization as a core competency.

When we are engulfed by a crisis, we are forced to draw on our reserves: the human capabilities, values, and physical resources we have built over time. Building resilience is a set of deliberate acts you can take as a leader to strengthen those reserves. It's mostly too late to try and develop them in the middle of a crisis. The fundamental issue here is one of *readiness*.

The key is to build and maintain readiness while things are still going well. This is as true at the individual level as it is at the organizational level. As the lesson of the sigmoid curve teaches us in Chapter 7, the single biggest cause of failure is the way we deal with success. Failure is seldom caused by what the environment does to us. It is caused more often by what we do to ourselves.

There is a tendency in human conduct to relax our vigilance, to loosen our grip, when times are good and the living appears easy. Chess masters have learned that their moment of greatest vulnerability is immediately after a big struggle in which they have gained an advantage, and the threat of defeat seems to have receded. The result is a temporary lapse in concentration and resolve that is often their undoing.

Organizations that are successful over the long haul understand and apply these principles. Continuously building resilience, strengthening fundamentals, and enhancing readiness, in good times and bad, is part of their DNA. They never blow hot and cold on these things. And, notably, these sturdy companies are able to weather the inevitable storms when they come along, and emerge all the stronger for it.

ExxonMobil is an outstanding example of such a company. The oil industry has seen major changes over the years, from economic cycles to embargoes to expropriations, such as happened in Venezuela. Through all these vicissitudes, ExxonMobil has consistently outperformed its key competitors on its return on capital employed.

One of the biggest recent changes was totally unforeseen. The price of a barrel of oil rose dramatically from around $60 in mid-2007 to $147 in the summer of 2008. All previous assumptions were suddenly out of date. There were no market factors that could readily explain an increase of this magnitude and speed. It was unclear whether investor speculation may have been behind it. There were dire warnings from analysts that the price could rise to $200 a barrel and stay there, causing the industry to scramble to develop a fresh set of assumptions to guide investment policy. Then, suddenly, the price reversed course and dropped by 70 percent in a mere six months, to just over $40 by the end of 2008, the steepest drop ever in oil prices. (As of November, 2009, the price was hovering between $75 and $80 a barrel.)

Despite this extreme volatility, ExxonMobil was still able to generate an excellent profit in 2008, including positive results in the especially difficult fourth quarter.

How has ExxonMobil managed to create this state of built-in readiness to cope so successfully with unforeseen events? The answer: a steadfast commitment to a clear set of operating principles that are embedded in the organization's culture. The company has captured the vital elements of this operating philosophy in what amounts to a manifesto, a written statement called its Leadership Framework. The Leadership Framework contains this definition of what the organization calls its Fundamental Business Principles:

▼ Ethical behavior and strong business controls

▼ Unwavering commitment to operations integrity

▼ Disciplined, efficient use of capital

▼ Continuous focus on cost management

▼ Commitment to develop the highest-quality, motivated, diverse workforce

▼ Commitment to technology leadership

ExxonMobil's Leadership Framework is no idle statement. It is a way of life. It is constantly communicated and explained to every level in the organization. The framework is taught and reinforced on all the company's executive education programs. (I have had the honor over the past seven years to serve as the faculty director for the company's flagship program for its senior executives, the Global Leader Forum, which is run by Columbia Business School.) Living these values is built into the company's measurement and reward systems. Promotion to senior ranks is dependent on practicing these values and imbuing them in others. Perhaps most important, the leaders in the organization unfailingly serve as role models for these leadership behaviors, especially during difficult times.

Seizing Opportunities during a Crisis

Resilient companies have an ideal opportunity to enhance their competitive advantage during a crisis. The current recession is a case in point. It is the most severe economic downturn since the Great Depression. Many companies have seen their resources stretched to the limit. As a matter of survival, they have been forced to hunker down and conserve. In adverse conditions such as these, resilient companies have the benefit of a stronger relative resource base from which to compete.

Wal-Mart, the giant mass-merchandising chain, is a good example. Through thick and thin, Wal-Mart has strengthened its fundamentals, never being tempted into sloppiness or taking unwarranted risks. It has been a pioneer of great supply-chain management and has consistently generated higher inventory turnover than its competitors, thus giving the company a superior return on operating assets and a stronger cash flow.

The recession has hit retailing hard, as consumers have pulled back on spending. While most of its competitors are struggling to staunch losses, Wal-Mart's robust fundamentals have enabled it to not only withstand the downturn but at the same time to leverage its increased relative strength. It is investing an additional $1.6 billion in its campaign to upgrade its 3,600 U.S. stores, making it increasingly attractive to more affluent shoppers. And it is continuing to simplify its business by reducing the number of items in stores. This will result in less clutter, help the staff spend more time assisting customers, and, of course, further improve operating efficiencies. According to a report in *BusinessWeek* on June 15, 2009, "Wal-Mart reports higher sales, faster inventory turnover, and happier shoppers in remodeled stores."[2]

The Human Dimension

When all is said and done, how well an organization works its way through a crisis becomes a human question. Tom Watson, Jr., when he was head of IBM, said, "The basic philosophy, spirit, and desire of an organization have far more to do with its achievements than do technical or economic resources."[3]

The basic philosophy I have been discussing centers on ensuring readiness in an uncertain world. It involves building organizational adaptiveness through a sense-and-respond capability that we can rely on, both in good times and bad. It includes the need for rigorous business disciplines that continuously strengthen the organization's foundations and enhance its resilience. It means managing in the short term while looking to the long term.

Ultimately, all this needs to be crystallized and clearly expressed through an organization's belief system: the values and accompanying behaviors that represent its culture. These disciplines and values represent an organization's character and its moorings. They also make up the reservoir we draw from when we are tested by a crisis.

Tom Watson Jr. rightly adds the dimensions of "spirit and desire." Fear, uncertainty, and doubt are natural human reactions to a crisis. These factors, by themselves, can paralyze an organization's ability to deal successfully with the challenges involved. This is where effective leadership and constant communication become all-important. At times like these, leaders must be always visible, always explaining what is happening and what needs to be done, always encouraging the human spirit. It is critical that leaders take personal responsibility for the successes and failures of their organization, never portraying the company as a helpless victim of circumstances.

Total honesty is vital. Mostly the news is not going to be good, and dressing it up is demeaning both to leaders and their employees. Often there will be a need for pay cuts, downsizings, and layoffs. These inevitably involve a human toll, which affects not only those being let go but also the survivors. It is crucial to deal with these things honestly, respectfully, and fairly—no favorable treatment for the higher-ups. There is nothing more self-defeating than an organization pulling successfully through a crisis but emerging at the other end with its morale in tatters. In times of crisis, *how* leaders do things is just as important as *what* they do.

To be sure, there is no guaranteed formula about what it takes to become a long-lived organization. But I do think one of the responsibilities leaders owe themselves and the organizations they serve is to be explicit about their theory of success—the principles that will guide their actions.

I will stick my neck out and offer you my own, here. These are what I believe to be the five key rules for long-term success:

1. Clarity of focus
2. A unique point of difference that creates superior value for customers and stakeholders
3. A motivated workforce
4. Operational effectiveness, coupled with strong financial disciplines
5. The capacity for change and renewal

I have described these fundamentals in very simple terms, and that may make them look deceptively easy, even obvious. But I invite you to pause for a moment and consider them more deeply in the context of your own organization and your role within it. Construct a vivid mental picture of excelling at each one of these elements, individually and in combination, working powerfully together.

Remember, success happens twice: first in our minds, and then in the field of action. Now decide for yourself whether these are the success factors that will really count in making your organization resilient.

Becoming an Integrated Leader

The greatest help in meeting any problem with whatever courage is demanded is to know where you yourself stand. That is, to have in words what you believe and are acting from.

—William Faulkner

The real joy of teaching is that it is the greatest way on earth to learn.

When I first joined Columbia Business School in 1996, I was asked to teach a strategy course in the Executive MBA program. This was a really exciting opportunity for me. Because I had run multinational businesses over a period of 20 years, I felt I could bring practical examples and a pragmatic approach to the topic.

But the truth was that I was still a novice at the teaching game and had a lot to learn. What we owe our students is not just a series of war stories from our own experience but a sound conceptual foundation based on the best thinking from the various scholars in the field. I therefore dedicated myself to this goal, in itself a continuous journey of learning and discovery.

As the first semester went along, I realized that it felt just plain wrong to be teaching strategy as something separate from leadership. At almost every turn during class discussions, the connections between strategy and leadership were brought to light. This vital interrelationship was what I had also experienced as a CEO. A leader's role is largely integrative: to orchestrate the right combination of things. And no combination is stronger or more important than the interaction between strategy and leadership.

Ever since that time, my teaching and my writing have always emphasized that strategy is not an isolated subject. It is an inseparable part of leadership. That's why the Strategic Learning cycle is intentionally defined as a *leadership* process. While no leader can lead successfully without a winning strategy that provides focus, clarity, and meaning, it is equally true that a strategy, no matter how brilliant, will take an organization nowhere without the leadership capability to mobilize the commitment and creative energy of its people. It is the strategic and personal aspects working hand in hand that constitute what I call "integrated leadership," the key to leadership effectiveness. This chapter explores how to achieve this integration.

The Three Domains of Leadership

Integrated leadership results from the effective synthesis of the three key domains of leadership, as illustrated by the interlocking circles in Figure 11.1. All three must work together synergistically to achieve integrated leadership. If any one of the three domains is deficient, so is one's leadership.

Let's explore each of the three domains.

Intrapersonal Leadership: Leading Self

During the standard safety announcement on airlines before takeoff, we are told, "Put on your own oxygen mask before attempting to

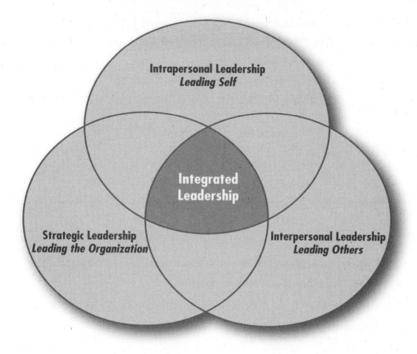

Figure 11.1 Strategy and Leadership: Essential Parts of Each Other

help others." In addition to being good practical advice, this is also a good metaphor for successful leadership. The essential starting point—the source material—of successful leadership is the effective leadership of self. If we do not attend to our own leadership "oxygen," we cannot expect to be successful in leading others.

Intrapersonal leadership is about being firmly anchored in who you are and what you stand for. It's about being clear on your values and consistently applying these to guide your life and your decisions. In the final analysis, it is about being genuine.

The successful leadership of self involves the following factors:

▼ A deep sense of self-knowledge.

▼ A set of morally sound values that clearly define who you are.

▼ The preparedness to stand up for what you believe in.

▼ Self-control combined with optimism.

▼ Commitment to a cause larger than yourself.

These elements establish authenticity and moral character. They are the foundation of one's ability—indeed, they are one's permission—to persuade and lead others.

Strategic Leadership: Leading the Organization

As discussed earlier, organizations create their future through the strategies they pursue. The essential role of strategic leadership is to provide a clear sense of direction that will enable an organization, its people, and its stakeholders to prosper.

Strategic leadership involves:

▼ Making sense of the changing environment.

▼ Using these insights to determine where to compete, how to win, and what priorities to pursue.

▼ Applying the right disciplines for effective implementation.

▼ Ensuring the organization is financially sound.

▼ Building the organization's capacity for change and renewal.

Each of the elements described here can be mobilized by applying the Strategic Learning process. But, as I have emphasized, the final product of a strategy is not a document. While a clearly documented strategy is an essential discipline, a strategy document by itself does not represent leadership. Rather, it provides the *platform* for leadership: the basis for energizing your people in support of what needs to be done.

Interpersonal Leadership: Leading Others

Interpersonal leadership involves the ability to win the hearts and minds of others.

Mobilizing collective effort in support of an organization's strategy has always required strong skills in motivation, team building, and persuasion. In today's increasingly multicultural teams, these skills are required more than ever. Furthermore, organizations are now often structured as a matrix, blurring the formal lines of reporting.

Strict command-and-control systems are largely a thing of the past. Attempting to rely solely on positional power is a symptom of leadership failure. The key to success is the ability to influence others without formal authority—peers, subordinates, and superiors. Interpersonal leadership encompasses:

▼ Translating your strategy into a simple, compelling leadership message.

▼ Fostering collaboration and teamwork.

▼ Showing appreciation for the perspectives, feelings, and concerns of others.

▼ Overcoming resistance and inspiring commitment.

▼ Creating a high-performance culture based on shared values and a common purpose.

Leadership effectiveness is achieved when these three domains are integrated, each enhancing the others. No one of them can succeed without the support of the other two.

Articulating Your Leadership Credo

At Columbia Business School we have developed a vehicle for integrating the three domains of leadership, which we call the Leadership Credo. The Leadership Credo is a succinct statement of a leader's personal beliefs and leadership principles, the vision and strategy of the organization, and the shared values of the enterprise that will drive success.

Every Leadership Credo is unique, but should provide compelling answers to the following questions:

1. *What do I stand for as a leader?* What are the principles and personal values that clearly define who you are and guide your approach to life and to leadership? Identify your three to five core values and reflect on the "stories" in your life and career that have helped to shape them. Draw on the lessons you have learned from your own accomplishments, setbacks,

relationships, and turning points, or from observing the world around you. The stories of these moments can help you articulate these values for yourself and explain them to others.

2. *What is our organization's vision and how will we win?* A leader must be able to communicate a vision that serves as a unifying goal and provides meaning for the daily tasks of employees. This is the concept of the "cathedral" that we discussed in Chapter 8. In addition, it is important to clarify how the organization will reach its goal by summarizing the Winning Proposition, Key Priorities, and highlights of the implementation plans. The aim is to provide a brief but compelling summation of the organization's vision and strategy by crystallizing the *why*, *what*, *how*, and *how much*.

3. *What do we stand for as an organization?* What are the shared values and behaviors that will help drive our success as an organization? Describe the key values—no more than five—and related behaviors that will form the foundation of the organization's culture. The culture must be directly aligned behind the organization's strategy as a powerful force to help drive it forward. It is important that you not only clarify these key values and explain their importance but that you serve as a personal example of these values in action.

Questions 2 and 3 of the Leadership Credo relate to the definition of the strategic direction of your organization and the specific norms and behaviors that describe its culture. The answers to these questions will vary depending on the particular challenges and situations your organization faces. Prior chapters of this book explain how the Strategic Learning process can help you construct your answers.

Constructing the answer to question 1, however, depends on the essence of who you are, a constant that you carry with you wherever you go. Because this intrapersonal aspect of leadership is the threshold requirement for the other two domains, I would like to explore it more fully.

The Quest for Self-Knowledge

Very few of us ever achieve perfect self-knowledge. It has been said that when there are two men in an elevator, there are really six men present: each one as the other sees him; each one as he sees himself; and each one as he actually is. How do you integrate all these perceptions into one true reality?

I'm reminded of a story about the origins of the word *sincere*, which I learned from reading *The Leader's Voice* by Boyd Clarke and Ron Crossland.[1] In ancient Rome, they explain, statuary was the ultimate status symbol. Dishonest sculptors would cover flaws in their work with wax to deceive the viewer. But over time, the sun, wind, or rain would expose all the imperfections. Artisans with integrity refused to follow this practice and proudly displayed a sign reading "*sine cera*," or "without wax." Sculptors who worked *sine cera* guaranteed the real thing.

A good leader is *sine cera*, without wax. What you are is what you show, without pretenses. Deep self-knowledge is a gift you give yourself. It is an inner journey, a lifelong quest to define your values that no one else can undertake for you. The reward is authenticity.

Principles are easy to apply when there are no trade-offs. The test of authenticity is being prepared to stand up for what you believe in, despite the hard knocks that may result. As Albert Camus pointed out, our life's journey is the sum of the choices we make. The most important choice we make is choosing the principles by which we will choose our actions. Being authentic is when our principles and our deeds are totally consistent.

Many people know of the golfer Bobby Jones for his winning record as a player. He deserves equal accolades for his sportsmanship. In the 1925 U.S. Open, Jones was getting set to hit a shot out of the rough when he felt his club accidentally touch the ball and move it a tiny fraction of an inch. He gained absolutely no advantage and no one else saw him touch the ball, but Jones called a one-stroke penalty on himself. He went on to lose the championship—by one stroke. When spectators praised him, he dismissed their accolades. "There is only one way to play the game of golf," he replied. "You might as well praise me for not robbing a bank."[2]

There is an interesting question that sometimes comes up in my executive programs: "Can leadership be taught?" My own view is that strategic leadership and interpersonal leadership can be taught. There are concepts and frameworks that can help us improve our skills in these two leadership domains. But intrapersonal leadership is different. It cannot be taught in the same way; but it can be *learned*. I agree with Margaret Wheatley's assessment that, "We cannot change a living system from the outside. We can only disturb it so that it changes itself."[3]

There is great benefit in doing the necessary self-examination to make our values explicit. We cannot hope to explain our values to others unless we have first explained them to ourselves. We are human, of course, and we will sometimes fall short of the values we choose to live by. But our learning and growth come from knowing where we fell short.

The Lifeline Exercise

If someone were to ask you stone-cold, "What are the key values that define who you are?," you would probably find it rather difficult to answer on the spur of the moment. Our values are deep inside us somewhere, and they guide our everyday behaviors (unless we simply act capriciously). However, being able to articulate them clearly so they honestly reflect who we are is not so easy.

We need a method for reflection and self-discovery, a way to think deeply about our life's experiences and how these have shaped what we believe in and who we are. During leadership programs at Columbia Business School, we often use a useful approach called the Lifeline Exercise.

Here's how it works: Draw a line across a sheet of paper. This is a timeline representing your life from birth up to the present. Next, insert check marks with brief descriptions of the major events and key turning points in your life. In one way or another, these watershed moments have helped define who you are and what you believe in. They may include achievements, disappointments, and crises that you have experienced or witnessed.

Now, translate this timeline into a story. It's the story of your life, if you like. Reflect on this story and identify the moments of truth that have shaped the person you are today. What lessons did they teach you? What values emerged from them that guide the way you live and the way you lead?

Share this story with a trusted colleague, then reverse the process and listen to your colleague's story. By telling your story and answering questions from your discussion partner, you deepen your own understanding of yourself. Listening to your colleague's story allows you to practice empathy and enlarge your understanding of your shared humanity.

By making your life's lessons and the values you have derived from them explicit, the Lifeline Exercise can be a liberating and insightful experience. When I did this exercise, I became acutely aware of two major influences on my life.

The first of these was a patriotic act by my father. During World War II, there was no conscription in my native South Africa; signing up to fight for the Allies was purely voluntary. In 1942, Hitler's armies appeared to have the upper hand. Yet my father decided to leave his young family (my sister was 10, and I was only 5) and serve a cause he believed in. I vividly remember watching his train pulling away from the station, as he started off on his long journey to Europe. None of us could be sure he would return. Even then, I was aware that he was doing this for the simple reason that he believed it was *right*.

Mercifully, my father returned safely in 1945. Looking back, one great lesson endures for me. The example set by my father taught me the crucial difference between purely physical courage and moral courage. The former involves doing daring but morally neutral things—like skydiving. The latter involves acting on a core principle, and accepting the risks involved, as my father and millions of others did.

Often the risks incurred in exercising moral courage are not physical. They may relate to factors such as popularity, career advancement, power, or wealth. Regrettably, we have all seen people of acknowledged physical courage fail to stand up for principle and truth when the chips are down. Ever since childhood, I have regarded moral courage as a true gauge of character, and have strived to live my life accordingly. Nothing grieves me more when I look back on any event in my life than the sense that I may have fallen short of this yardstick.

The second defining influence was growing up and spending my early career in South Africa during the apartheid era. As a small child I took apartheid for granted. This was the world as I found it, and there was plenty of "indoctrination" to provide a moral-sounding construct for this inhuman policy. As I grew older, I began to realize that there was something profoundly wrong with this state of affairs, and in my university days I took part in numerous protests.

But apartheid's effects became agonizingly real for me when, as a young lawyer in Cape Town, I took on a number of cases on behalf of individuals who had been classified as "colored" rather than white. There was an odious piece of legislation called the Race Classification Act that gave a government board the power to classify people's race according to a set of visual and cultural criteria. Because the races were segregated by law, this finding would determine where someone could live and go to school, what work they could do, with whom they could have sexual relations, which public toilets they could use, and so on. The application of this law reached new depths when individual members of the same family were classified differently, or when a courting couple was classified differently and therefore prohibited from marrying. The appeal process required the aggrieved individuals to submit themselves to a degrading personal inspection, whereby the board members would examine them as if they were laboratory specimens, go through the checklist of criteria for assessing their whiteness or nonwhiteness, add up the score, and pronounce their verdict. The indignities and human distress involved have haunted me ever since.

This wrenching experience instilled two important personal values within me. The first is to be fair, and stand up for fairness toward others. The second is to respect the personal dignity of all human beings.

I have lived in America since 1980 and have become an American citizen. In 1994, I was deeply moved to watch the moment on television when South Africa became a multiracial democracy.

Gradually, the scar of the apartheid era is healing as South Africa moves forward under its new constitution, which guarantees equality and basic human rights for all its citizens.

These were two major moments of truth from my lifeline. Each individual will have his or her own story to tell, his or her own lessons learned.

Learning from the Example of Others

It is not just from our own lives that we learn and grow. We can also find wisdom and inspiration from the lives of others. Their stories help us learn to define our values.

I am personally inspired by two life stories in particular: Albert Einstein, the famous physicist, and the psychiatrist Viktor Frankl, who survived the horrors of a Nazi concentration camp. Both men achieved great things. But what I admire just as much is their capacity for reflection and self-knowledge. It is for these reasons that I offer their examples here.

In 1931, Albert Einstein published a simple article called "The World as I See It."[4] In it, he offered his beliefs and values. Here is an excerpt:

> How strange is the lot of us mortals! Each of us is here for a brief sojourn; for what purpose he knows not, though he sometimes thinks he senses it. But without deeper reflection one knows from daily life that one exists for other people— first of all those upon whose smiles and well-being our own happiness is wholly dependent, and then for the many, unknown to us, to whose destinies we are bound by ties of sympathy. A hundred times every day I remind myself that my inner and outer life are based on the labors of other men, living and dead, and that I must exert myself in order to give in the same measure as I have received and am still receiving.

Viktor Frankl's remarkable book, *Man's Search for Meaning*, chronicles his experiences as an inmate at Auschwitz and other concentration camps.[5] He pondered why some inmates survived the starvation, unimaginable physical cruelty, and degradation while others succumbed and died. Some of his reflections are quoted here:

> We who lived in concentration camps can remember the men who walked through the huts comforting others, giving away their last piece of bread. They may have been few in number, but they offered sufficient proof that everything can be taken from a man but one thing: the last of the human freedoms—to choose one's attitude to any given set of circumstances, to choose one's own way. . . . Between stimulus and response, there is a space. In that space is our power to choose our response. In our response lies our growth and freedom.

As these two examples show, the essence of effective leadership starts from the inside, with a deep and secure knowledge of self. Its foundation is a set of firmly held and clearly expressed values that form the basis for all actions, thus giving the leader authenticity—wax-free sincerity, if you will. Only then can we effectively apply the other two domains of leadership.

Applying Strategic Learning to Yourself

The development of ourselves as integrated leaders requires a process of lifelong learning and growth. When I considered this truth, the following question arose: could the underlying concepts of Strategic Learning, which offers demonstrable benefits to organizations, also be used to develop leadership effectiveness in individuals? In other words, could this same four-step process be as useful a tool for personal growth as it is for organizational renewal?

I am convinced that the answer is yes. After all, learning is at the heart of both strategy creation and leadership development. The only difference is that strategy creation involves an outside-in learning process, starting with an understanding of customers and the competitive environment, whereas leadership development involves inside-out learning, starting with an understanding of self. Like an

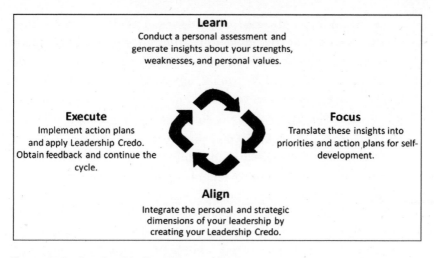

Learn
Conduct a personal assessment and generate insights about your strengths, weaknesses, and personal values.

Execute
Implement action plans and apply Leadership Credo. Obtain feedback and continue the cycle.

Focus
Translate these insights into priorities and action plans for self-development.

Align
Integrate the personal and strategic dimensions of your leadership by creating your Leadership Credo.

Figure 11.2   Leadership Development Cycle

adaptive organization, an adaptive individual must continually learn and translate that learning into action.

The four steps of Strategic Learning can be translated into a personal Leadership Development Cycle as shown in Figure 11.2.

Over the past eight years, the Leadership Development Cycle has been systematically applied in our executive programs at Columbia Business School, both with companies such as Ericsson, Deloitte, ExxonMobil, and Novartis, as well as with numerous participants in our open enrollment programs. The results have been truly exciting.

Executives find that the process is a powerful way for them to develop greater self-knowledge and to leverage this for personal development. They particularly value the fact that it is a simple tool that they can use for themselves as a vehicle for lifelong learning. And, most important, it has helped them effectively integrate strategy and leadership.

The four basic steps of the process are applied like this:

1. *Learn.* Conduct a personal Situation Analysis through an honest self-appraisal and by getting feedback from those around you. Use tools such as the Lifeline Exercise, 360-degree feedback, and executive coaching to generate insights about your

personal strengths and weaknesses. Develop clarity about the values that are most important to you. Examine your environment—that is, the business and industry in which you work and the role you occupy—and identify the specific leadership challenges you face.

2. *Focus*. Translate your newfound insights about your strengths and weaknesses, your personal values, and the leadership challenges you face into a set of priorities and action plans for self-improvement— your Winning Proposition. What are the most important strengths you need to build on? What are the key weaknesses that need improvement? What are the gaps that you need to close? Concentrate on those competencies that contribute most to leadership effectiveness.

Consider how the personal values you identified in the Lifeline Exercise will sustain and guide you in the leadership challenge you currently face. Finally, develop a short list of no more than five personal development priorities, together with specific actions you will take and a method for assessing your progress.

3. *Align*. This is the crucial step for integrating the personal and strategic dimensions of your leadership. The Leadership Credo is the vehicle for achieving this integration. This requires answering the three basic questions:

▼ What do I stand for as a leader?

▼ What is our organization's vision and how will we win?

▼ What do we stand for as an organization?

4. *Execute*. This is the learn-by-doing step in the cycle. Implement your personal improvement plan. Articulate your Leadership Credo at every opportunity. Continually appraise your own performance, seek feedback, and use it as the basis for further learning and improvement.

As always with Strategic Learning, the key is to repeat the cycle again and again. You should never stop learning. Unfortunately, many promising managers derail their careers when they stop striving for self-improvement, either because they think they've learned all there is to know or because they fail to translate their learning into meaningful leadership development.

The keys are to keep yourself open to new ideas and self-examination, to work with truth-tellers you can trust to give you honest, unbiased feedback about your strengths and weaknesses, and to use the Leadership Development Cycle as a process for incorporating what you learn into your daily practice.

The world looks to integrated leaders to solve the problems, large and small, that confront us in civil society, in our governments, and in our various institutions, whether they are commercial or not-for-profit organizations. Strategic leadership is a vital part of this, but it is not enough. To achieve its full power, strategy must work in combination with the intrapersonal and interpersonal aspects of leadership.

I believe that leadership has a moral dimension and that the development of a sound set of values, grounded in authenticity, helps us rise to what we can be.

When the subject of values comes up in classes or in my consulting work, I like to cite the following folk wisdom:

A Native American elder was teaching his grandchild about life. "A fight between two wolves is going on inside me," he said. "One wolf represents fear, anger, envy, regret, greed, arrogance, self-pity, resentment, lies, false pride, and ego. The other stands for joy, peace, love, hope, sharing, serenity, humility, kindness, friendship, generosity, truth, compassion, and faith. This same fight is going on inside you and inside every other person."

"Which wolf will win, grandfather?" the child asked.

The elder replied, "The one you feed."[6]

CONCLUSION

THE FIVE CS: CHOICES, CLARITY, CHANGE, COURAGE, AND COMPASSION

W e need to reinvent the way we think about strategy. A dynamic (VUCA) world demands that we meet the challenge with dynamic concepts and processes. The old, static "strategy as planning" methods no longer work. We must shift gears to an agile "strategy as learning" approach.

The new mission of strategy is to create adaptive enterprises capable of sustaining competitive advantage by sensing and rapidly responding to change on a continuous basis. The logic is essentially Darwinian: The key to long-term survival is to generate favorable variations, those that confer a competitive advantage. However, unlike nature's random mutations, the imperative for organizations is to *learn* their way to renewal.

Learning is a competitive pursuit. Sensing patterns and trends earlier and more clearly than competitors produces a crucial advantage. It is the gateway to opportunity. Winning the contest for the best insights is where the competition really begins.

But insight must lead to action. A strategy must produce a very specific output that represents that call to focused collective effort. In a world where customers and investors have choices, the goal of an organization is to win the competition for value creation—customer value and economic value. Thus, the key output of a strategy is a Winning Proposition: *what an organization will do differently or better than its competitors to deliver greater value to its customers and superior financial returns for the enterprise*. This holds true for both commercial and not-for-profit institutions. Without a clearly defined Winning Proposition (not a mere Value Proposition), an organization cannot claim to have a strategy.

But in an ever-changing environment, winning once is not enough. To survive and thrive, an organization must go on winning.

The necessary consequence is that strategy and planning are two different undertakings, requiring separate but linked processes: strategy first and planning afterward. To mix them together in one process almost always shortchanges strategy and undermines an organization's ability to think and function strategically.

On the other hand, strategy and leadership are essential parts of each other, and the one cannot work without the other. In the final analysis, every failure of strategy is a failure of leadership, either to set the right direction for the organization or to mobilize the energy and commitment of employees in support of what needs to be done.

There is an outdated idea that strategy is something created at the top of an organization and that everyone else's job is simply compliance—the "command and control" notion that the top thinks and the bottom acts. This is not a successful philosophy.

Because it is about winning at value, strategy is everyone's job at each level in an organization. Every leader in the system must start with a clear line of sight to the organization's overall vision and strategy, and then *translate* that into an aligned Winning Proposition and Key Priorities within his or her own domain of responsibility. For the total enterprise to win at value, each part of the organization must contribute to that superior value. We should get rid of the notion of a "cost center." Every subgroup in an organization should function as a "value center," with a Winning Proposition and Key Priorities that support the total effort.

The Five Cs

The major themes of strategy and leadership that we have been discussing can be distilled into these five touchstones.

Choices

"All things to all people" is the original recipe for failure. Success comes from the ability to create an intense focus on the few things that matter most. Maximum power is achieved through focus multiplied by compounding.

This requires making stark choices that define what you will do and what you will *not* do. When you choose something, you have to give up something. Choice-making involves sacrifice.

The choices that will determine your destiny are deciding where you will compete, what you will offer your intended customers, and how you will win the competition for value creation. These choices represent the heart of your strategy.

The goal is to outsmart your competitors. Therefore, competitive rivalry begins with the battle for superior insights. The best insights will equip you to make the best choices.

Clarity

Complexity paralyzes an organization. In a turbulent and confusing world, a crucial leadership competency is the ability to simplify, to strip things down to their simple essence so they can be grasped and acted on by everyone in the enterprise.

Devising a winning strategy is not enough. To galvanize an organization, that strategy must be translated into a compelling leadership message that wins the hearts and minds of employees. Logical arguments alone will not win the day. Human beings are engaged and motivated through stories, metaphors, and pictures that enliven their imagination. Great leaders are great storytellers.

Effective communication is not a one-time event. It is an ongoing campaign. For a message to be understood and acted on, it must be endlessly repeated, and the leader must embody the message.

Ultimate clarity comes from providing meaning to everyday tasks. To repeat Nietzsche's dictum, "People will do almost any *what* if you give them a good *why*." Effective leaders provide a vivid description of "the cathedral" that everyone is helping to build.

Change

The environment is in a state of constant flux. It will not stand still for us. The long-term success of organizations will depend on their ability to sense and rapidly respond to change on a continuous basis. Doing that better than competitors is the only sustainable competitive advantage available to us.

Research shows that organizations must change while they are still successful, that if they wait until they begin to fail, their chances of renewal will decline rapidly. Paradoxically, the single biggest cause of failure is the way organizations deal with success.

Change is destabilizing. There is thus a natural tendency for individuals and organizations to cling to the past. The biggest test of leadership is to sense when change is necessary, and then successfully convert resistance into active support for the change that is needed.

Courage

Strategic Learning is designed to help organizations think and function strategically. But the process is an aid to leadership, not a substitute for it. In the end, the value it delivers is a function of leadership effectiveness—the ability to integrate the strategic and personal elements of leadership.

Leadership requires courage: the courage to confront reality and make tough choices; to admit mistakes and learn from them; to lead change in the face of resistance; to tell the truth when it is unpalatable; to do the right thing when it is more profitable not to; to stand up for principle above expediency.

Leadership is not a safe haven. You will never have "enough" information to make a risk-free decision. Chasing after the missing

10 percent is usually a fool's errand. And you will never know in advance whether your strategy will succeed.

Courageous leaders are optimistic, and they spark enthusiasm in others. They are committed to a cause greater than themselves. For them, leading is not about power. It is about service. They also have the humility to understand that they achieve nothing on their own. They are dedicated to fostering teamwork and leaving behind a stronger talent base than the one they inherited.

Compassion

We are reminded by Confucius that, "If you want to be a leader, you must first be a human being."

Change inescapably extracts a human toll. Leaders are judged as much by *how* they deal with human issues as by *what* they do.

Successful leaders possess empathy. They are sensitive to the needs, concerns, and expectations of their people. They are resolutely fair. They embrace diversity. They unfailingly preserve the dignity and self-respect of everyone on the team, as well as those whom they must ask to leave the organization.

Some might see courage and compassion as contradictory. I suggest that the opposite is true. Indifference is easy. It takes moral courage to be compassionate.

*   *   *

Our challenge, of course, is to convert these ideas into action. The way that concerted action is achieved in an organization is through a systematic process that is deeply embedded in the culture. A piecemeal, ad hoc approach is not sufficient. In Chapter 3, I quoted Marco Pierre White's famous dictum about the importance of a disciplined process. He pointed out the negative consequences of not applying such a process. Let's convert his statement into its positive counterpart: *Simplicity creates clarity, clarity creates consistency, and consistency creates success.*

Strategic Learning offers a practical process that helps organizations implement the ideas I have outlined in this book, simply, clearly, and consistently. It is a dynamic, learning-based method for creating and implementing winning strategies on an ongoing basis. Its unique feature is that it unifies strategy, learning, and leadership in one holistic, mutually reinforcing process that helps organizations adapt promptly and effectively to changes in the competitive environment.

To adapt is to learn and grow. This applies with equal force to organizations and to individuals. Thus, the same four steps in the Strategic Learning Cycle also apply to the development of individual leaders: *Learn*, *Focus*, *Align*, and *Execute*. The key difference is that strategy is an outside-in process, while leadership development is an inside-out process. The threshold requirement for leadership effectiveness is a deep knowledge of self.

Let me emphasize that Strategic Learning is not a silver bullet nor a mechanical process. It is designed to mobilize the leadership concepts that underlie it. Its value lies in the quality of the outputs that are derived from it, not from just going through the motions. Its aim is to enhance an organization's ability to think and function strategically and thereby to build its leadership capacity.

I have been inspired by the successful application of Strategic Learning by many organizations, large and small, commercial and not-for-profit. Two things have stood out clearly.

> The first is that the level of success is invariably determined by the commitment of the leaders in the organization. Instilling a new process in an organization involves a belief in its value and a dedicated effort to achieve the necessary simplicity, clarity, and consistency to make it work.

> The second is the huge payoff of deliberate practice. We cannot become great at something by doing it once. The first effort will never be our best, and will take us longer to complete. Just like champion athletes, organizations get better and faster at an activity through training and repetition. Closing the doing/excelling gap means constantly learning your way to greater and greater success.

APPENDIX

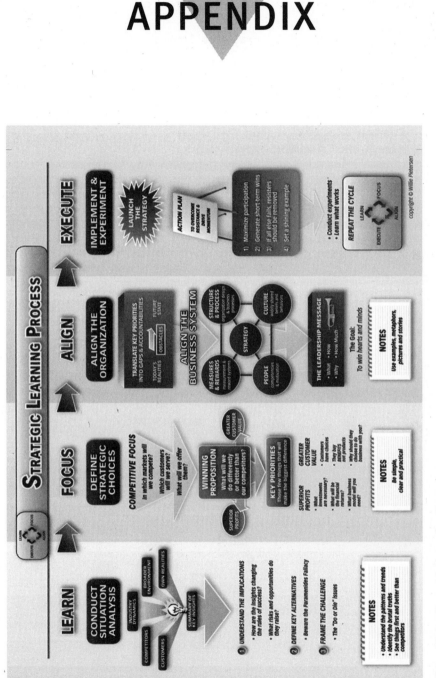

Figure A.1 Strategic Learning Process

Implementing the Strategic Learning Process

Core Strategy Team: + − 25 Executives (5 teams)

<u>Kickoff Workshop</u> : <u>(1 Day)</u>
• Review Process
• Brief Teams on Situation Analysis

↓   4 to 6 Weeks

<u>Strategic Choices Workshop</u> : <u>(2–3 Days)</u>
• Review and Crystallize Situation Analysis
• Agree Competitive Focus, Winning Proposition, Key Priorities

↓   4 Weeks

<u>Alignment and Implementation Workshop</u> : <u>(2 Days)</u>
• Create draft gap statements and appoint gap champions
• Agree alignment plan
• Define the leadership message

Figure A.2   Implementing the Strategic Learning Process

NOTES

Introduction

1. Daniel Pink, *A Whole New Mind*, pp. 49–50 (New York: Penguin Group, 2005).

Chapter 1

1. Johnathan Katz, "Employees Unaware of Company Strategies." *IndustryWeek*, February 13, 2006.
2. Stephen Covey, *The 8th Habit: From Effectiveness to Greatness*, pp.2–3 (New York: Simon & Schuster, Inc., 2004).
3. Edward E. Lawler III and Christopher G. Worley, *Built to Change*, p. 1 (San Francisco: John Wiley & Sons, Inc., 2006).

Chapter 2

1. Art Kleiner, "Pankaj Ghemawat: The Thought Leader Interview," *Strategy + Business*, Spring 2008, www.strategy-business.com.
2. Norman C. Berry, "Revitalizing Brands," *The Journal of Consumer Marketing*, Summer 1988, p. 16.
3. Warren Buffett as quoted by Janet C. Lowe, *Warren Buffett Speaks*, p. 99 (New York: John Wiley & Sons, Inc., 1997).
4. "GM assumes 19%-plus U.S. market share, director says," *Reuters*, October 15, 2009, http://europe.autonews.com.
5. Steve Lohr, "All May Not Be Lost for the American Car," *The New York Times*, January 31, 2009, www.nytimes.com.

Chapter 3

1. Robert Lloyd quoting Marco Pierre White, "The Chopping Block," *Los Angeles Times*, March 11, 2009, www.latimes.com.
2. "Changes ExxonMobil has Made to Prevent Another Accident Like Valdez?" www.exxonmobil.com/corporate.
3. Frederick Winslow Taylor, *The Principles of Scientific Management*. (New York: Harper & Brothers Publishers, 1911).
4. Henri Fayol, *The Bulletin de la Société de l' Industrie Minérale, printed his Administration, Industrielle et Générale – Prévoyance, Ogranisation, Commandement, Coordination, Contrôle, 1916*, translated by Constance Storrs in *General and Industrial Management*. (London: Pitman Publishing, 1949.)
5. Michael Porter, "How Competitive Forces Shape Strategy," *Harvard Business Review*, March–April 1979, pp. 137–145.
6. Charles Darwin, *On the Origin of Species*. (New York: Random House, Inc., 1993, first published 1859).
7. Arie de Geus, "Planning as Learning," *Harvard Business Review*, March–April 1988, p. 71.
8. W. Edwards Deming, *Out of Crisis*. (Boston: The MIT Press, 2000).
9. Will Durant quoting Aristotle in *The Story of Philosophy: The Lives and Opinions of the Greater Philosophers*. p. 98 (New York: Simon & Schuster, 1926).
10. K Anders Ericsson, Michael J. Prietula, and Edward T. Cokely, "The Making of an Expert," *Harvard Business Review*, July–August 2007, pp. 115–121.
11. Ibid.
12. Ibid, p. 119.

Chapter 4

1. Peter Drucker, "The Theory of the Business," *Harvard Business Review*, September–October 1994, p. 95.
2. Ian Davis and Elizabeth Stephenson, "Ten Trends to Watch in 2006," *The McKinsey Quarterly*, January 2006, www.mckinseyquarterly.com.
3. Sun Tzu, translated and interpreted by Ralph D. Sawyer, *The Essential Art of War* (New York: Basic Books, 2005).
4. Eugene Ionesesco, Découvertes (1970), as quoted by Stuart Wells, *Choosing the Future: The Power of Strategic Thinking*, p. 15 (Massachussets: Butterworth-Heinemann, 1997).

5. William Gibson as quoted by Paul Saffo, "Six Rules for Effective Forecasting," *Harvard Business Review*, July–August 2007, p. 127.

6. Henry Ford as quoted by Nancy F. Koehn, "Steve Job's Legacy," *Fortune*, November 2009, www.cnnmoney.com.

7. A.H. Maslow, "A Theory of Human Motivation," *Psychological Review* 50(4) 1943:370–96.

8. Tzu, translated and interpreted by Ralph D. Sawyer, *The Essential Art of War* (New York: Basic Books, 2005).

9. Jim Cappa, "Gold," *Rocktalk* 6 no. 2, www.geotech.org.

10. Paul Saffo, "Looking Ahead: Implications of the Present," *Harvard Business Review*, September 1997, p. 30.

11. Mike McConnell interviewed on Charlie Rose, January 8, 2009, http://www.charlierose.com/view/interview/9903.

12. Albert Szent-Gyorgyi quoted in I.J. Good, *The Scientist Speculates*, p. 15 (New York: Basic Books, 1963).

13. Dr. Maretha Prinsloo, Magellan Consulting, summary of research furnished to author, November 20, 2009.

14. Brian Greene, "That Famous Equation and You," *New York Times*, September 30, 2005, www.nytimes.com.

Chapter 5

1. Roger Enrico as quoted by Jeffrey E. Garten, *The Mind of the CEO*, p. 147 (New York: Perseus Books Group, 2002).

2. Philip Bobbitt, "Today's War is Against Tomorrow's Iraq," *New York Times*, March 10, 2003, www.nytimes.com.

3. Christopher Palmeri, "Sysco's Hands-On Way of Keeping Restaurants Going," *BusinessWeek*, May 7, 2009, www.businessweek.com/magazine.

4. Robert Southey as quoted by William Matthews, *Oratory and Orators*, p. 100 (Boston: Adamant Media Corporation, 2006).

5. Howard Schultz, "What I Know to Be True," *Transformation Agenda Communication #4*, February 4, 2008, www.starbucks.com.

6. Richard Koch, *The 80/20 Principle: The Secret to Success by Achieving More with Less*, p. 16 (New York: Doubleday, 1998).

Chapter 6

1. Frederick Henderson as quoted by John D. Stoll and Sharon Terlep, "GM Takes New Direction," *The Wall Street Journal*, July 11, 2009, p. B1.

2. GE 2004 Annual Report, Letter to Stakeholders, "Developing a Generation of Growth Leaders," accessed at www.ge.com also found in "Growth as a Process," *Harvard Business Review*, June 2006, pp. 67–68.
3. Robert Slater, *Saving Big Blue*, p. 93 (New York: McGraw-Hill, 1999).

Chapter 7

1. Will Durant, *Caesar and Christ*, p. 665 (New York: MJF Books, 1944).
2. Charles Handy, *The Age of Paradox*, pp. 50–67 (Boston: Harvard Business School Press, 1994).
3. Howard Gardner, *Changing Minds: The Art and Science of Changing Our Own and Other People's Minds*, p. 56–57 (Boston: Harvard Business School Publishing, 2006).
4. Lew Platt as quoted by Viv Shackleton, *Business Leadership*, p. 118 (London: Thomson, 1995).
5. Jack Welch, *GE 2000 Annual Report*, p. 4, www.ge.com.
6. Andrew Martin, "At McDonald's, the Happiest Meal is Hot Profits," *New York Times*, January 11, 2009.
7. Ibid. See also http://retailsails.com and www.reuters.com.
8. Margaret Thatcher as quoted in "Notable and Quotable," *Wall Street Journal*, http://online.wsj.com (accessed October 6, 2009).

Chapter 8

1. Howard Gardner, *Five Minds for the Future*, p. 7 (Boston: Harvard Business School Publishing, 2006).
2. Richard T. Pascale, Mark Millerman, and Linda Gioja, *Surfing the Edge of Chaos*, p. 136 (New York: Three Rivers Press, 2000).
3. William Shakespeare, *Julius Caesar*, Act I Scene 2, line 147.
4. George Bernard Shaw as quoted by Marlene Caroselli, *Leadership Skills for Managers*, p. 71 (New York: McGraw Hill Publishers, 2000).

Chapter 9

1. Ellen Byron, "Tide Turns 'Basic' for P&G in Slump," *Wall Street Journal*, August 6, 2009.
2. Jeffrey Pfeffer and Robert I Sutton, *The Knowing-Doing Gap: How Smart Companies Turn Knowledge into Action*, pp. 15–23 (Boston: Harvard Business School Press, 2000).

3. Professor Takahiro Fujimoto as quoted by Alex Taylor III and Jeremy Kahn, "How Toyota Defies Gravity," *Fortune*, December 8, 1997, http://money.cnn.com/magazines/fortune.
4. Larry Huston and Nabil Sakkab, "Connect and Develop: Inside Proctor and Gamble's New Model for Innovation," *Harvard Business Review*, March 2006, p. 60.
5. Tim Brown, *Change by Design: How Design Thinking Transforms Organizations and Inspires Innovation*, p. 218 (New York: Harper-Collins, 2009).
6. Marilyn Darling, Charles Parry, and Joseph Moore, "Learning in the Thick of It," *Harvard Business Review*, July 2005, pp. 84–92.

Chapter 10

1. Daniel Patrick Moynihan quoted by Robert A. Katzmann, *Daniel Patrick Moynihan: The Intellectual in Public Life* (Baltimore: The Johns Hopkins University Press, 1998).
2. Matthew Boyle, "Wal-Mart Moves Upmarket," *BusinessWeek*, June 3, 2009, www.businessweek.com/magazine.
3. Tom Watson, Jr. as quoted Thomas J. Peters and Robert H. Waterman, *In Search of Excellence*, p. 280 (New York: HarperCollins, 1982).

Chapter 11

1. Boyd Clark and Ron Crossland, *The Leader's Voice: How Your Communication Can Inspire Action and Get Results!*, p. 108 (New York: SelectBooks, 2002).
2. Craig Lambert quoting Bobby Jones, "Bobby Jones: Brief life of a golf legend: 1902–1971," *Harvard Magazine*, March 2002, www.harvardmagazine.com.
3. Margaret J. Wheatley and Myron Kellner-Rogers, *A Simpler Way*, p. 49 (San Francisco: Berrett-Koehler Publishers, Inc., 1996).
4. Albert Einstein, *Living Philosophies*, p. 3–7 (New York: Simon Schuster, 1931).
5. Viktor E. Frankl, *Man's Search for Meaning*, pp. 65–66 (Boston: Beacon Press, 1959).
6. Art Horn, *Beyond Ego: Influential Leadership Starts Within*, p. 3 (Toronto: ECW Press, 2008).

INDEX

AAR. *See* After-action review (AAR)
Adaptive enterprise, application of
   strategic learning to create
   alignment, 41, 43, 109–133 (*See also*
     Alignment *for detailed*
     treatment)
   complexity theory, 39
   execution, 41, 43, 171–179 (*See also*
     Execution *for detailed*
     treatment)
   Five Forces model, 37
   focus, 40–41, 43, 81–107
     (*See also* Focus *for detailed*
     treatment)
   insight, 40
   key steps, 33–45
   killer competencies, 40–41
   leadership message, 157–170
   learning, 43, 47–80 (*See also*
     Learning *for detailed treatment*)
   learning organizations, 39–40
   natural selection, 37–38
   new mission of strategy, 40
   ongoing adaptation, 36
   practice, deliberate, 43–45
   renewal, cycle of, 41

   resistance to change, overcoming,
     135–155 (*See also* Resistance to
     change, overcoming *for detailed*
     treatment)
   retention, 38
   robust method, 34–35
   selection, 38
   strategic learning cycle, 41–42
   thought processes, 35–37
   variation, 38
Adler, Deborah, 57–59
After-action review (AAR), 177–179
Airbus, 8–10, 67
Air France, 9
Airline industry. *See also specific*
   airline
   competitive advantage, 19–20
Alignment, 41, 43, 109–133
   business ecosystem, 119–125
   business ecosystem and skills,
     124–125
   gap, closing, 113–119
   golden rules for successful
     execution, 112–113
   implementation, keys to successful,
     113

Alignment (*continued*)
  key priorities, 114
  leadership, 110–111
  MTI (managing things in isolation), 119
  organizational culture, business ecosystem, 124
  organizational culture, changing, 125–131
  R&D, 122–123
  self, application of strategic learning to, 208
  and successful execution, 112–113
  values trap, avoiding, 131–133
ALPO, 169
Analyzing Customer Needs, 51
Apartheid, 154–155, 204–205
Aristotle, 43, 171
Arithmetic of business, 92
Army, U.S. *See* United States Army
Army War College, 162–163
Arthur Andersen, 55
Atomic bomb, 75–76, 84–85
Auschwitz, 205–206

Bannister, Roger, 114
Bechtel, 179
Beers, Charlotte, 146
Behavior
  business ecosystem, 124–125
  and leadership message, 161
Benchmarks, performance trends, 94–95
Big Four accounting firms, 54–56
Big Three (Detroit), 133
Binary thinking, 62
Bobbitt, Philip, 84
Boeing, 8–10, 67
Boston Consulting Group, 71
Bottom lines, 93–95
British Airways, 9
British Petroleum, 179

Broader environment, guiding questions, 68–69
Brown, Tim, 177
Buffett, Warren, 21
Business ecosystem, 119–125
  adjustments, 123–124
  and attitudes, 124–125
  and behaviors, 124–125
  competency model, 124
  culture, 124
  efficiency versus innovation organization, 122
  measures and rewards, 123
  people, 124
  R&D, 122–123
  and skills, 124–125
  structure and process, 123–124
Business Week, 191

CALL. *See* Center for Army Lessons Learned (CALL)
Camus, Albert, 3, 201
Cantalupo, James, 144
Cash flow, 93–95
Cathedral building example, leadership message, 161–162
Cemex, 20
Center for Army Lessons Learned (CALL), 178
Change, 214
  resistance to (*See* Resistance to change, overcoming)
Change by Design (Brown), 177
Changing Minds: The Art and Science of Changing Our Own and Other People's Minds (Gardner), 141
China Mobile, 69
Choice-making, 8–12
Choices, 213
Citrus Hill, 64–65
Clarity, 213–214
Clarke, Boyd, 201

Clear Rx, 57–59

Clinton, Bill, 155

Cloninger, Kathy, 99–102, 127, 143, 170

Coca-Cola, 68, 86, 133

Columbia Business School, 27–28, 162, 167

  Executive education program, 89

  Executive MBA program, 195

  lifeline exercise, 202–206

Columbia University, 77

  Global Leader Forum, 190

"Command and control," 212

Commander's intent concept, 162–163

Commitment versus consensus, 148–149

Communication, clarity, 213–214

Compassion, 215

Competencies

  business ecosystem, competency model, 124

  killer competencies, 40–41

Competitive advantage, defining, 15–29

  achieving competitive advantage, 17

  elastic band analogy, 18–21

  gap, 16–18

  "showdown" meetings, 27–29

  value and costs, 19, 23

  Winning Proposition of organization, 15, 24–29, 42

Competitors

  analyzing, 63–66

  guiding questions, 63–66

Complexity, 34, 39

Concorde, 9

Confucius, 215

Confusion, 34

Consensus, commitment versus, 148–149

Consumer Health Group, 135–136

Core values, 132

Costs, value and, 23

  elastic band analogy, 19

Courage, 214–215

Covey, Stephen, 4

Crisis, leading through, 183–193

  human dimension, 191–193

  learning way out of, 186–188

  opportunities, seizing during crisis, 190–191

  readiness, building, 188–190

  speed learning, 187

  unexpected, dealing with, 184–186

Crossland, Ron, 201

Cuban missile crisis, 75–76

Culture. *See* Organizational culture

Customers

  guiding questions, 51

  hierarchy of needs, 55

  understanding, 56–59

Darwin, Charles, 33, 37, 38

de Geus, Arie, 39

Deficiency needs, 54

Deliberate practice, 43–45

Deloitte, 54, 56

Deming, W. Edwards, 42–43, 96

Disaggregation, 72

  map, 71

Diversity and situation analysis, 49

Documentation of strategy, 159–160

Doing/excelling gap, closing, 14

Dreamliner, 9

Drucker, Peter, 37, 47, 48, 104

Durant, Will, 15

EBIT, 95

Efficiency versus innovation organization, 122

80/20 rule, 96–97, 114

Einstein, Albert, 106–107, 205

Elastic band analogy, competitive advantage, 18–21

Enrico, Roger, 83
Enron scandal, 55, 139
Ericsson (company), 56, 58, 123
Ericsson, K. Anders, 44
E. Snell & Co., 72
Essence of strategy, 12
Execution, 41, 43, 171–179
  after-action review (AAR), 177–179
  experiential learning, 177–179
  experimentation, learning through, 172–175
  mistakes, learning from, 176–177
  others, learning from, 175–176
  self, application of strategic learning to, 208
Experiential learning, 177–179
Experimentation, learning through, 172–175
ExxonMobil, 139
  Leadership Framework, 189–190
  Safety Protocol, 34, 107

Faulkner, William, 195
Fayol, Henri, 36–37
Federal Home Loan Bank (FHLB) of Atlanta, 184–187
Feeling and leadership message, 160
FHLB. *See* Federal Home Loan Bank (FHLB) of Atlanta
Five Cs, 213–215
Five Forces model, 37
Five Minds for the future (Gardner), 160
"Five Ps," 145
Florida State University, 44
Focus, 40–41, 43, 81–107
  arithmetic of business, 92
  bottom lines, 93–95
  cash flow, 93–95
  competitive focus, 82
  deciding what not to do, 103–107
  EBIT, 95
  80/20 rule, 96–97

gearbox parable, 97–98
geranium story, 103–106
Girl Scouts of the USA (GSUSA), 99–102, 127, 143
  key priorities, 82, 83, 95–99
  Parmenides Fallacy, 83–87, 105
  performance trends, 94–95
  profits, delivering superior, 90–93
  return on assets (ROA), 93–95
  return on equity (ROE), 95
  return on invested capital (ROIC), 95
  return on sales (ROS), 93–95
  self, application of strategic learning to, 208
  strategic choices, 81–83
  subtracting and multiplying, 106–107
  unequal distribution principle, 96–97
  Value Proposition versus Winning Proposition, 87–89
  vision, 90
  Winning Proposition, 82, 93–95
The Fog of War (documentary), 75
Ford, Henry, 53
Fortune 1000 companies, 4–5
Fortune Top 20, 139
Four-minute mile, 113–114
Frankl, Viktor, 205–206
Fujimoto, Takahiro, 174–175

Gap
  closing, through alignment, 113–119
  competitive advantage, defining, 16–18
  defining, 115
  doing/excelling gap, closing, 14
Gardner, Howard, 141, 160
GE. *See* General Electric
Gearbox parable, 97–98
General Electric, 139
  AAR, 179
  England factory, 20
  values, 130, 132

General Motors
    decline of, 21–24, 26, 126, 139, 143
    and energy-efficient cars, 76
Geranium story, 103–106
Gerstner, Lou, 126–128, 131
Gibson, William, 53
Girl Scouts of the USA (GSUSA), 99–
        102, 127, 143
    in immigrant communities, 164–165
    key priorities, 116–119
    leadership message, 170
    organizational culture, 128
    strategic priorities, 102
    Winning Proposition, 100, 102
Gladwell, Malcolm, 99
Globalization, 175
Global Leader Forum, 190
GM. *See* General Motors
Golden rules for successful execution,
        112–113, 136
Golfers, 44
Good Housekeeping Institute, 58
Google, 26
Great Depression, 190
Greene, Brian, 77
Greer, Kyle, 136, 137
Grove, Andy, 85–86
GSUSA. *See* Girl Scouts of the USA
        (GSUSA)
Guiding questions
    broader environment, 68–69
    competitors, 63–66
    customers, 51–59
    industry dynamics, 66–68
    own realities, facing, 69–73
    situation analysis, 49–56, 50–56
    stakeholders, 59–63

Hallmark Cards, Inc., 26
Hamel, Gary, 183
Harvard Business Review, 175
Healthcare industry, 60–61
Henry Schein, Inc., 123

Hewlett-Packard, 141
Hierarchy of needs, 53–55
Hiroshima, 84–85
Hitachi, 20
Hitler, Adolph, 203
Honda, 22–23
Honesty, 192
The how, 166
The how much, 167
Human dimension in crisis,
        191–193
Huston, Larry, 175–176

IBM, 86, 123, 126–128, 191
IDEO, 34, 177
Immigrant communities
    Girl Scouts of the USA (GSUSA),
        164–165
Implementation
    alignment, 113
    strategic learning process,
        illustration, 217
Industry dynamics, 66–68
Information and insight, differences,
        73
Insight, 40, 75–78
    and information, differences, 73
    synthesis, 76–78
Institute for Safe Medicine Practices,
        58
Institute for the Future, 26
Instrumental values, 132
Integrating leadership and strategy
    becoming integrated leader, 195–209
    crisis, leading through, 183–193
Intel, 85–86
International oil companies (IOCs), 60
Internet, 69, 175
Interpersonal leadership, 198–199
Intrapersonal leadership, 196–198
IOCs. *See* International oil companies
        (IOCs)
Ionesco, Eugene, 51

Japanese companies, 84–86
Jobs, Steve, 166
Jomini, Antoine, 8
Jones, Bobby, 201
Julius Caesar (Shakespeare), 164
Juran, Joseph, 96

Key priorities, 95–99
 alignment, 114
 80/20 rule, 114
 focus, 82, 83
 Girl Scouts of the USA (GSUSA),
  101–102, 116–119
 leadership message, 164
Killer competencies, 40–41
Koch, Richard, 96

Landy, John, 114–115
Leadership. *See also* Leadership
 message
 and alignment, 110–111
 becoming integrated leader, 195–
  209
 and change, 111
 and courage, 214–215
 and crisis (*See* Crisis, leading
  through)
 defined, 160–161
 domains of, 196–199
 focus, 82, 208
 interpersonal leadership, 198–199
 intrapersonal leadership, 196–198
 leadership credo, articulating,
  199–200
 and learning, 207–208
 lifeline exercise, 202–206
 lifeline exercise, learning from
  example of others, 205–206
 organization, leading, 198
 self, application of strategic
  learning to, 206–209, 208
 self-knowledge, quest for, 201–202
 and strategic learning cycle, 82

and strategic learning cycle,
 situation analysis, 48
and strategy, illustrated, 197
Leadership and strategic learning
 cycle
 adaptive enterprise, 42
 alignment, 110
 execution, 172
 leadership message, 158
 resistance to change, 137
 self, application of strategic
  learning to, 207
Leadership message, 157–170
 behavior, 161
 cathedral building example,
  161–162
 commander's intent, 162–163
 definition of leadership, 160–161
 developing, 165–167
 documentation of strategy, 159–160
 and employees' questions, 165
 feeling, 160
 the how, 166
 the how much, 167
 key priorities, 164
 and repetition, 169–170
 and storytelling, 167–169
 thinking, 160
 the what, 166
 the why, 166, 214
The Leader's Voice (Clarke and
 Crossland), 201
Lean Enterprise Institute, 22
Learning, 43, 47–80
 Analyzing Customer Needs, 51
 broader environment, 68–69
 competitors, analyzing, 63–66
 crisis, learning way out of, 186–188
 customer hierarchy of needs, 55
 deficiency needs, 54
 and diversity, 49
 guiding questions, 50–56
 hierarchy of needs, 53–55

importance of learning, 211
industry dynamics, 66–68
insight, 73, 75–78, 76–78
and leadership, 42, 48, 82
process, 50
pulling together, 73–74
realities, facing, 69–73
reinvesting learning, 107
self, application of strategic
    learning to, 207–208
"sense and respond" imperative,
    48–49
situation analysis, 48–56
society as ultimate stakeholder,
    61–63
and stakeholders, 59–63, 61–63
successful, 78–80
understanding customers, 56–59
Learning organizations, 39–40
Lego, 26
Lifeline exercise, 202–206
    example of others, learning from,
        205–206
The Living Company (de Geus), 39

Mandela, Nelson, 154–155
Man's Search for Meaning (Frankl),
    205–206
Martin, Andrew, 145
Maslow, Abraham, 53–55
McDonald's, 144–146
McKinsey, 48
McNamara, Robert, 75
Mistakes, learning from, 176–177
Moynihan, Daniel Patrick, 188
MTI (managing things in isolation),
    119
Murphy, Julie, 116–119
Museum of Modern Art, 58

National oil companies (NOCs), 60
National Training Center, 178
Natural selection, 37–38

New York Times, 145
NGOs, 62
Nietzsche, Friedrich, 157, 163, 214
Nike, 86
NOCs. *See* National oil companies
    (NOCs)
NSA. *See* U.S. National Security
    Agency (NSA)
NUMMI, 133

Ogilvy and Mather, 146
Oil industry, 60
Ongoing adaptation, 36
Only the Paranoid Survive (Grove),
    85
Opportunities, seizing during crisis,
    190–191
Organizational capabilities, 37
Organizational culture
    alignment, 124–131
    business ecosystem, 124
    changing, 125–131
    culture-building, 126
    high-performance culture, defined,
        129–131
    measuring, 128–129
Organization, leading, 198
Others, learning from, 175–176
    execution, 175–176
    lifeline exercise, 205–206
Own realities, facing, 69–73

Pareto, Vilfredo, 96, 114
Parmenides Fallacy, 83–87, 105, 142
Participation, maximizing, 146–149
    commitment versus consensus,
        148–149
PepsiCo, 68, 83, 133
Performance trends, 94–95
PGA Tour, 44
Planning, difference from strategy,
    12–14, 34
"Plan to Win" (McDonald's), 145

Platt, Lew, 141
Porter, Michael, 37
Portfolio Probability Map, 71
Practice, deliberate, 43–45
Prescription drugs, 57–59
Proctor & Gamble, 64–65, 139, 175
    experimentation, Tide Basic, 173
Proust, Marcel, 47

Questions, guiding. *See* Guiding
    questions

R&D, 104, 122–123, 175–176
Readiness in crisis, building, 188–190
Renewal, cycle of, 41
Repetition, 169–170
Resistance to change, overcoming,
    135–155
    commitment versus consensus,
        148–149
    dealing directly with resisters,
        150–154
    example, setting, 154–155
    growth and discovery, 139
    incrementalism, focus on, 142
    inward-looking organizations, 141
    maturity, 139–140
    mental models, frozen, 140–141
    participation, maximizing, 146–149
    and politics, 141
    risk-aversive organizations, 142
    second curve, launching, 142–146,
        143
    short-term wins, generating, 149–
        150
    sigmoid curve, 138–139, 143
    sources of resistance, dealing with,
        137–138
    and success, 139–142
Retention, 38
Return on assets (ROA), 93–95
Return on equity (ROE), 95
Return on invested capital (ROIC), 95

Return on sales (ROS), 93–95
Right Management Consultants, 4
ROA. *See* Return on assets (ROA)
Robust method of strategy creation,
    34–35
ROE. *See* Return on equity (ROE)
ROIC. *See* Return on invested capital
    (ROIC)
ROS. *See* Return on sales (ROS)

Sakkab, Nabil, 175
SAP, 18
Shechtman, Steve, 64–65
Seagram USA, 150–153
Second curve, launching, 142–146
Selection, 38
Self-knowledge, quest for, 201–202
Seneca, 81
"Sense and respond" imperative,
    48–49
Shakespeare, William, 164
Shell Oil, 39
Short-term wins, generating, 149–150
"Showdown" meetings, 27–29
Sigmoid curve, 138–139
    second curve, launching, 143
Singapore Airlines, 19–20, 20
Situation analysis, 48–56
    customer hierarchy of needs, 55
    deficiency needs, 54
    and diversity, 49
    and Girls Scouts of the USA,
        99–100
    guiding questions, 49–56, 50–56
    hierarchy of needs, 53–55
    process, 50
    pulling together, 73–74
    successful, 78–80
Skinner, James, 144, 145
Snead, Sam, 44
Social organizations, 138
Society as ultimate stakeholder, 61–63
Socrates, 51

Software industry, evolution of, 52–53
South Africa
  Apartheid, 154–155, 204–205
Southey, Robert, 89
Speed learning, 187
Stakeholders, 59–63
  guiding questions, 59–63
  society as ultimate stakeholder,
    61–63
Storytelling and leadership message,
    167–169
Strategic choices, 81–83
Strategic learning cycle, 41–42
Strategic Learning Model, 85
Strategic learning process,
    illustration, 217
  implementation, 218
Strategic planning, 34
Strategy, defined, 5–6, 14
Strategy, overview, 3–14
  choice-making, 8–12
  definition of strategy, 5–6, 14
  doing/excelling gap, closing, 14
  essence of strategy, 12
  key questions, 6–8
  planning, difference from strategy,
    12–14, 34
Subtracting and multiplying, 106–107
Success
  and alignment, 112–113
  situation analysis, 78–80
Sun Tzu, 49, 63
Synthesis, 76–78
Sysco, 88–89, 123
Szent-Gyorgyi, Albert, 76

Target, 58
Taylor, Frederick Winslow, 36–37
Telecommunications, 56
Tewari, Ash, 80, 170
Texas, University of, 84
Thatcher, Margaret, 148
Thinking and leadership message, 160

Thought processes, 35–37
Tokyo University, 174
Transparency, 62
Tropicana, 64, 67–68
Truman, Harry, 84–85
Truth and Reconciliation
    Commission, 155
Twain, Mark, 70, 105, 135

Understanding customers, 56–59
Unequal distribution principle, 96–97
Unexpected, dealing with, 184–186
United States Army, 177–179
  Center for Army Lessons Learned
    (CALL), 178
U.S. National Security Agency (NSA),
    75

Value and costs, 23
  elastic band analogy, 19
Value Proposition versus Winning
    Proposition, 87–89
Values
  core values, 132
  instrumental values, 132
Values trap, avoiding, 131–133
Variation, 38
Virgin Atlantic, 19–20, 20
Vital Few, 96
VUCA (volatile, uncertain, complex
    and ambiguous), 36
  and change, 144
  demands of, 211
  and effective strategic leadership,
    14
  success in, 4

Wall Street Journal, 65
Wal-Mart
  crisis, during, 190–191
  supply chain management, 34
Watson, Tom, Jr., 191–192
Welch, Jack, 144

The what, 166
Wheatley, Margaret, 202
White, Marco Pierre, 33–34, 97, 107, 215
Who Says Elephants Can't Dance?
   Inside IBM's Historic
   Turnaround (Gerstner), 126–127
The why, 166, 214
Windex, 25
Winning, importance of, 7
Winning Proposition
   bottom lines, 93–95
   defined, 87, 212
   focus, 82, 87–93

Girl Scouts of the USA (GSUSA),
   100, 102
of organization, 15, 24–29, 42
and profits, delivering superior,
   90–93
and storytelling, 169
Value Proposition versus Winning
   Proposition, 87–89
Winthrop, Sterling, 135–136
Womack, James, 22
Woods, Tiger, 107
"The World as I *See* It" (Einstein),
   205
World War II, 84–85, 203, 205–206